Retro Camera Buying Guide

etting Serious
bout Photography
On the Cheap

by
Shawn M.
Tomlinson

Retro Camera Buying Guide

Getting Serious About Photography ...on the cheap!

ISBN: 978-1-329-31474-0

All photographs by Shawn M. Tomlinson that appear in this work were taken using four cameras recommended here:

Pentax *ist DS
Nikon D70
Canon EOS 10D
Sony A100

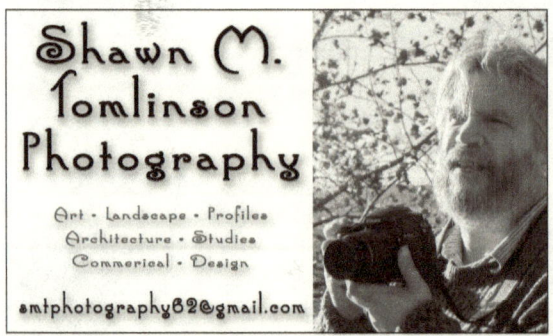

Shawn M. Tomlinson Photography

Art • Landscape • Profiles
Architecture • Studies
Commerical • Design

smtphotography82@gmail.com

Retro Camera Buying Guide
&
How to Pack
a Gadget Bag

Shawn M. Tomlinson's
Guide to Photography
Volumes 1 & 2

by

shawn m tomlinson

2015

Contents

Introduction to the Expanded Edition

My wife, Carole, wanted an eBook for her website about something to do with photography, as she put it.

So, I thought, why not put together a quick, step-by-step guide to packing a camera gadget bag for beginners. And, thus it came to pass... Ah, sorry.

Anyway, it was fun to do, so I decided to write a bigger eBook about buying older DSLR cameras. It's a fun way to get into more serious photography and, best, it's cheap.

Then I finally published eBooks about the author Robert W. Chambers after 37 years of research. Indirectly, that led to me reformatting and publishing the two photo eBooks on Amazon.com.

Ironically and typically, the photo guide books started selling far more than the Chambers books, and I liked writing them, so I wrote a bunch more.

To date, the gadget bag book has been my biggest seller on Amazon.

It always was my intention one day to publish these as actual, physical books, and here is the first one.

I decided to package the first two together because, well, the themes fit and the gadget bag book was a bit short on its own.

I hope that these books continue to be of use for budding photographers.

At least those with a sense of humor.

— Shawn M. Tomlinson
June 5, 2015
Ballston Lake, NY

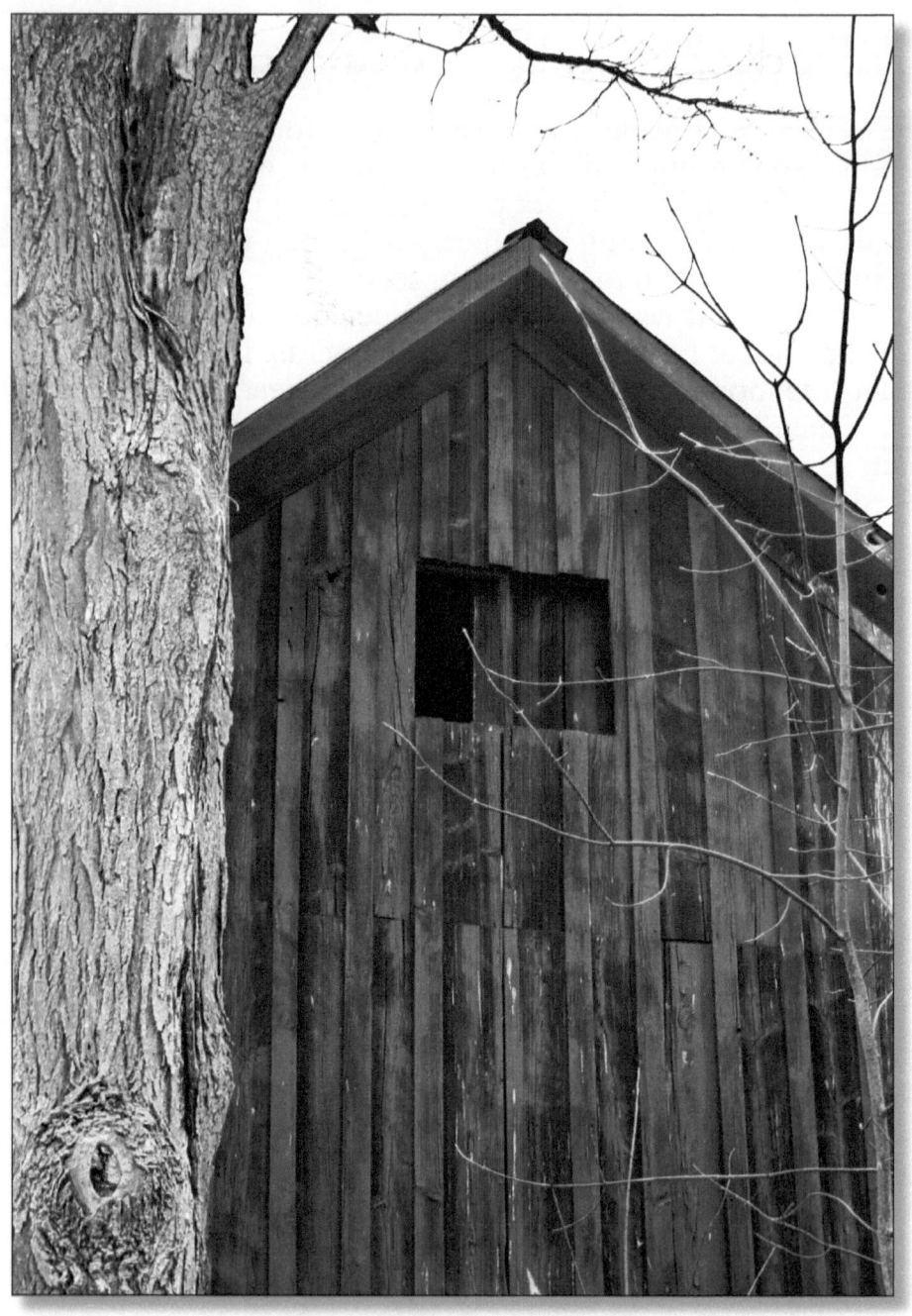

North Broadalbin, N.Y., April 4, 2014.
Canon EOS 10D, 57mm, f/4.5, 1/60, ISO 200, P, pattern metering.
© 2014, 2015 by Shawn M. Tomlinson

Part 1

Common Sense Photography

There's a Cold War going on in digital photography these days, and like the Cuban Missile Crisis, it is easy to get caught up in the frenzy and fear.

This war, concocted like that in *Citizen Kane*, is the product not of idealogical differences, but of propaganda that makes us want to fight.

Well, not fight, exactly, but at least drool over the next big thing in digital single-reflex cameras. It is, of course, the constant one-upsmanship of the megapixel battle.

Consumer-level DSLRs now have major megapixels a decade and a half ago only dreamed of. When

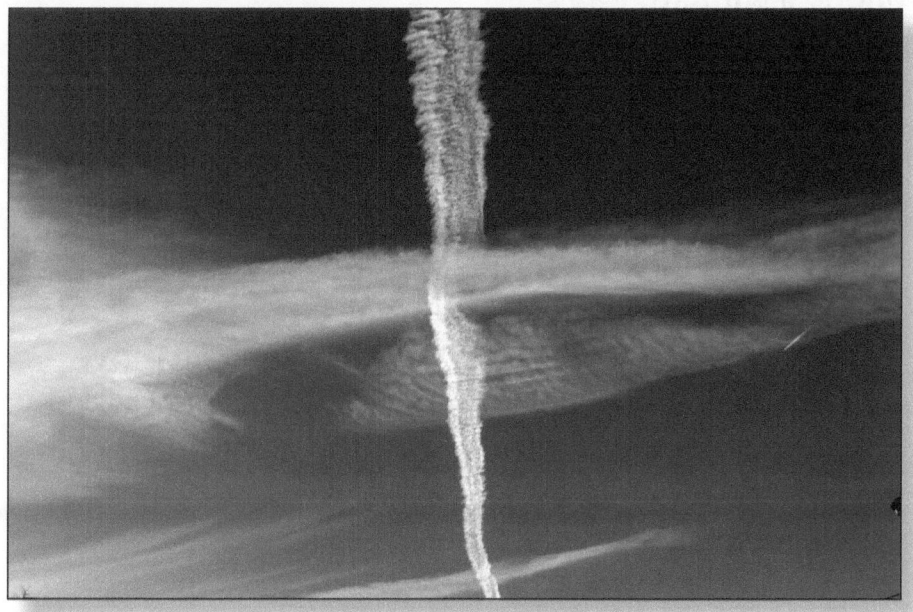

Amsterdam, N.Y., March 9, 2014.
Nikon D70, 70mm, f/13, 1/500, ISO 250, P, pattern metering
© 2014, 2015 by Shawn M. Tomlinson

Nikon introduced its D1 pro DSLR in 1999 it was a bargain at $6,000 with its whopping, unbelievably high resolution of 2.65 megapixels. As of 2014-15, you can get a 24-megapixel Nikon entry-level DSLR for around $700.

That's progress.

Well, sort of.

I used to buy into the megapixel Cold War myself and, OK, still would love to have that 36-megapixel Nikon D810, but it really is unnecessary.

I've proved this to myself.

Let's start, though, with some basics about you:

1) You *love* photography.

2) You're tired of the limitations of your smart-phone's camera.

3) You want to move into a little more serious photography.

4) You want to produce images as good as those on the web or in magazines.

5) You don't know where to start.

6) You're looking for help.

7) You don't have a lot of money.

Here, I'm going to show you that you can move into serious photography without a lot of money and how to get a good start on becoming a confident photographer.

So, let's go.

Camera Types

In digital photography, there are basically five types of cameras:

1) point-and-shoot
2) digital single-lens reflex
3) mirrorless
4) medium format
5) rangefinder

We're going to concentrate on the second one for several reasons.

Point-and-shoot cameras, as the term implies, are those little rectangular thingies you stuff in your shirt pocket or bag, whip out and snap a few snapshots.

There's nothing wrong with them, and as you move into this area of more serious photography, you may want to carry one as a second, easy-to-get-to camera. They really don't give you much control over your photos, however, so they really are mostly for snap-shots.

Mirrorless cameras are, essentially, single-lens reflex cameras without the mirror (reflex) and may be the wave of the future.

At this point, however, they still are relatively new.

That means they only will get better, but it also means they are more expensive.

Medium-format digital cameras, like medium-format film cameras were, are the choice of high-end

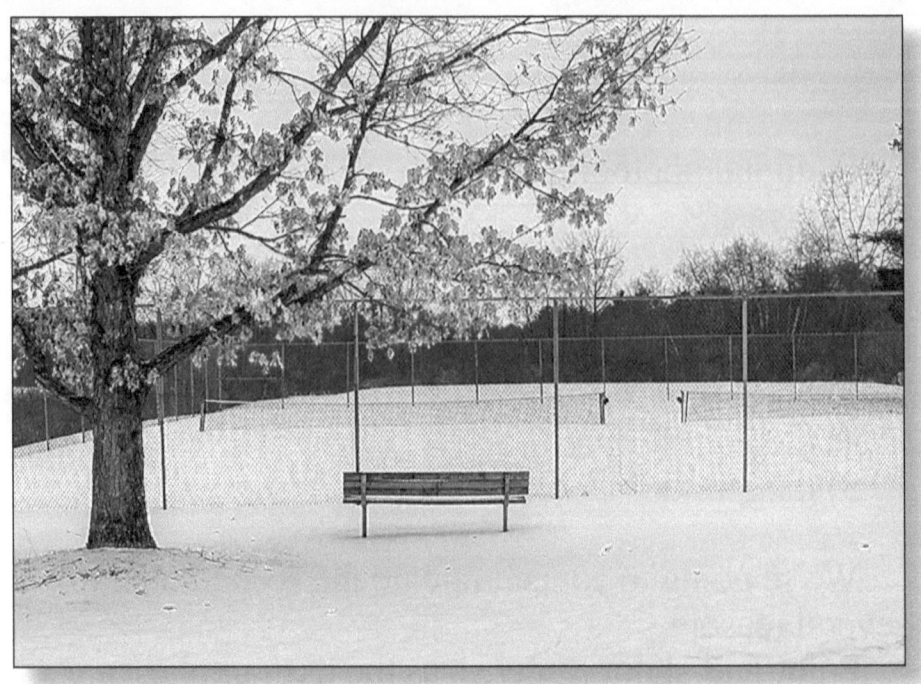

Indian Meadows Park, Glenville, N.Y., March 14, 2014.
Canon EOS 10D, 28mm, f/10, 1/250, ISO 200, P, pattern metering.
© 2014, 2015 by Shawn M. Tomlinson

studio photographers.

It is hard to beat — and no one has — the image quality from these cameras because of the cameras themselves, the advanced digital sensors and the incredibly good lenses made for them.

This all has a very high price, however. The standard, most well-known medium format camera, the Hasselblad, starts at around $30,000.

Rangefinder digital cameras are kind of an anachronism. Prior to the advent of single-reflex cameras, rangefinders, particularly those made by Leica, were the standard for pros.

Nikon introduced the first SLR system camera, the Nikon F, in 1959 and essentially took the rangefinder from most pros' hands.

Still, devotees have persisted and the rangefinder camera continued as a fringe, high-end tool. Somehow it managed to make it to digital, but I've never quite understood why. Except, of course, they use some of the best lenses made and tend mostly still to come from Leica, and those are terribly expensive. Not quite as pricey as Hasselblad, but up there.

Which leaves us with the standard for pros and serious amateurs alike:

The digital single-lens reflex camera, known from here on out as a DSLR.

This is the camera of choice, and it is the best way to break into more serious photography for not much money.

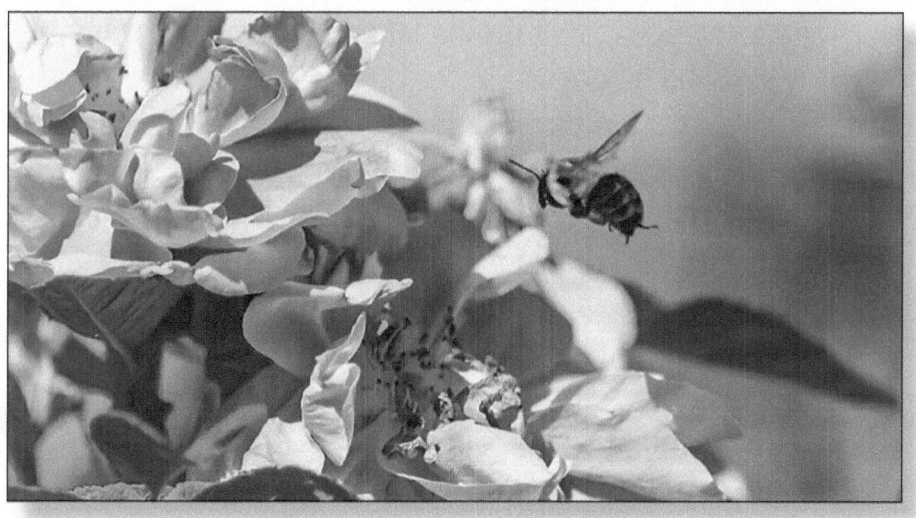

Central Park, Schenectady, N.Y., Aug. 17, 2014.
Nikon D70, 300mm, f/6, 1/6400, ISO 250, P, pattern metering
© 2014, 2015 by Shawn M. Tomlinson

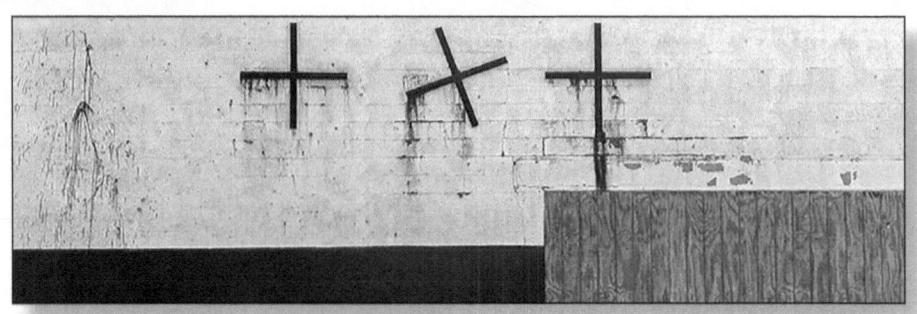

Terms

I know I'm throwing some terms around that might not be clear. They aren't always. For example, we call 35mm-style cameras SLRs or DSLRs, but medium-format cameras also are DSLRs. So let's clarify some terms quickly so we can move along.

1) Point-and-shoot camera: A small camera with a fixed lens, meaning you can't take the lens off without breaking it. Usually it will be a zoom lens, but it's the lens you're stuck with for the life of the camera.

2) Digital single-lens reflex camera: A camera designed in the same style as 35mm SLRs. It has a single lens that can be removed and replaced by various lenses for different uses and effects. It can do this because the lens that takes the photo is the same lens you see through.

The image comes in the lens, hits a mirror and bounces up into a pentaprism or pentamirror — which corrects the image left-to-right and top-to-bottom — and you see it almost exactly as it will appear in your recorded image. After you compose and focus the image, you press the shutter button, the mirror flips up out of the way, the sensor activates and records the image, then the mirror flips down again and you are ready for the next photo.

3) Mirrorless. A camera that acts the same was as a DSLR, except there is no mirror to flip up or down. It still has interchangeable lenses, but it is lighter and smaller.

4) Medium format: A camera that records a significantly larger image than any of the previous cameras. When it was film, a 35mm SLR took an image approximately 24-by-36mm, while a medium format camera usually shot an image 60-by-60mm. There were variations on this, but that's the average. This much greater film area gave the photographer sharper, bigger images that allowed greater enlargement. The same is true of digital medium-format cameras.

5) Rangefinder: A camera with a separate viewing and taking lens. The lens is coupled to two viewfinder windows, one on either side of the camera body. The two viewfinder windows allow a slightly different angle of the image. You turn the lens until the two superimposed images you see come together, meaning it is in focus.

A brand new and spiffy entry-level DSLR from Nikon, Canon, Pentax or Sony will cost you between $500 and $900 and usually will include a "kit" lens rated at 18-55mm. The resolution or image quality will range from 16 to 24 megapixels. This level of resolution is relatively meaningless, especially with the "kit" lens.

Even with today's costs, $500 to $900 is a lot of money for a DSLR camera body and not-so-great lens.

The point of this entire exercise is to save you money while providing the best images possible, so we

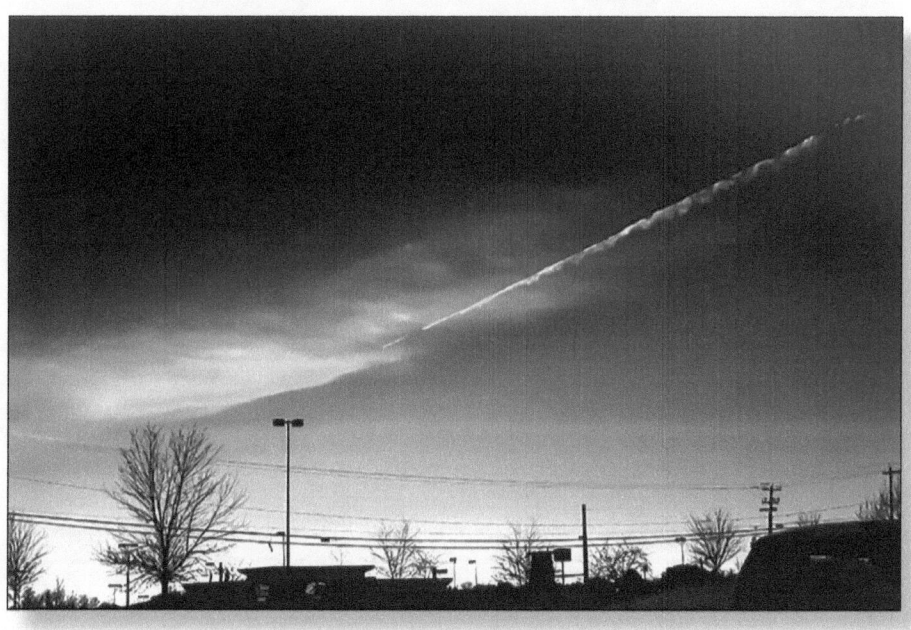

Amsterdam, N.Y., March 16, 2014.
Canon EOS 10D, 46mm, f/4, 1/750, ISO 200, P, pattern metering
© 2014, 2015 by Shawn M. Tomlinson

need to set a budget.

We're going to start at half the price for a new entry level DSLR kit, $250-$450. We can get an entire DSLR setup for that used from a reputable camera dealer, and start shooting great digital images immediately.

That $250 isn't just for some off-beat, no-name brand equipment, either. For that money, we can get a Canon, Nikon, Pentax or Sony DSLR body, a lens, a case and a UV filter that will put us well on our way to serious photography.

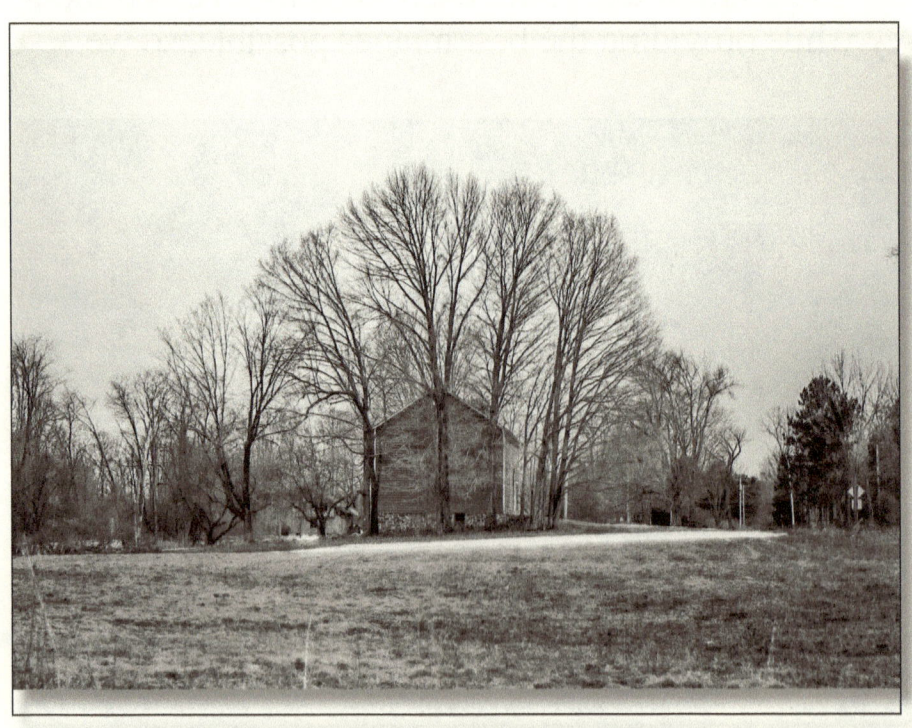

North Broadalbin, N.Y., April 4, 2014.
Canon EOS 10D, 38mm, f/4, 1/1000, ISO 200, P, pattern metering.
© 2014, 2015 by Shawn M. Tomlinson

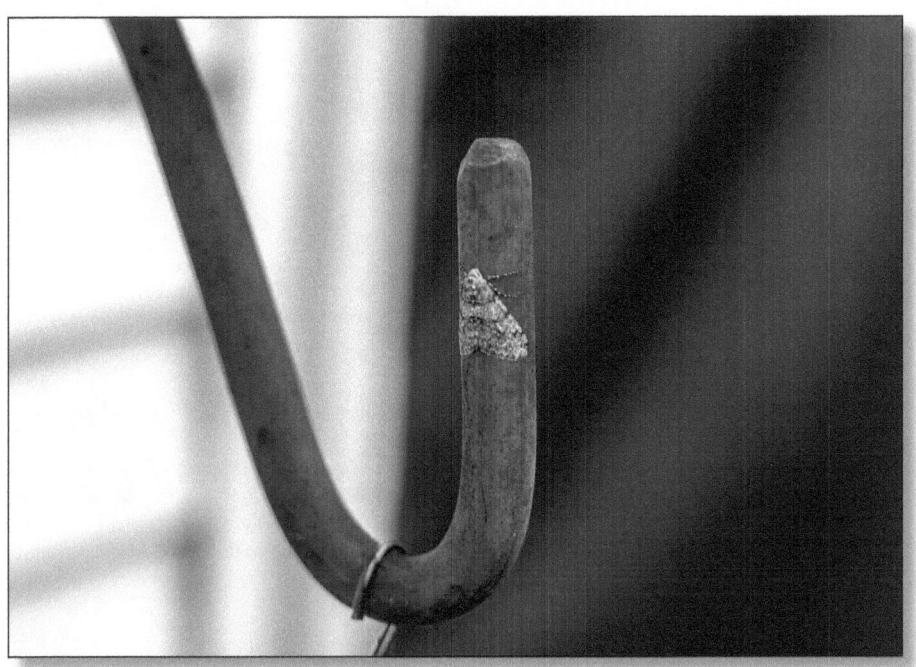

Ballston Lake, N.Y., April 10, 2015.
Sony A100, 50mm, f/3.5, 1/200, ISO 100, Tv, pattern metering.
© 2015 by Shawn M. Tomlinson

Megapixel Mania

Most photographers agree that between 6 and 10 megapixels is all anyone needs to make fantastic photos.

That doesn't make sense, right?

Why would camera makers keep touting higher and higher megapixel counts if it doesn't mean anything, right?

The answer is simple: They do it to keep you buying new DSLRs.

They need you to keep buying the newer model and ditching the last one in order to keep increasing profits. Sales have been dropping because most people are using their smartphones to take photos, not buying DSLRs.

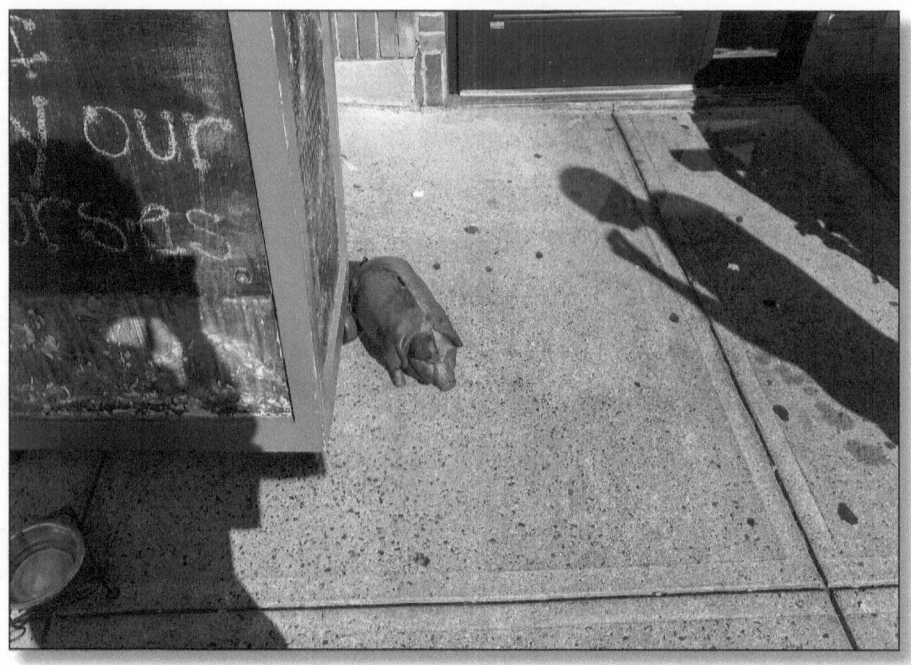

Saratoga Springs, N.Y., Aug. 2, 2014.
Nikon D70, 18mm, f/10, 1/400, ISO 200, P, pattern metering.
© 2014, 2015 by Shawn M. Tomlinson

They need to keep upping the megapixel count, but *you* don't.

The reasons photographers agree that 6 to 10 megapixels is plenty fall into two categories.

1) Most people never make prints larger than 8.5-by-11 inches. In fact, most people only print 4-by-6-inch photos when they print at all anymore.

At either of these sizes, 3 to 4 megapixels would be enough because you can't really see the grain or noise anyway. So, with 6 to 10 megapixels, these sizes will look sharp and render wonderful color.

2) High resolution requires better lenses. The 18-55mm lens that comes with most entry level DSLRs is great for most

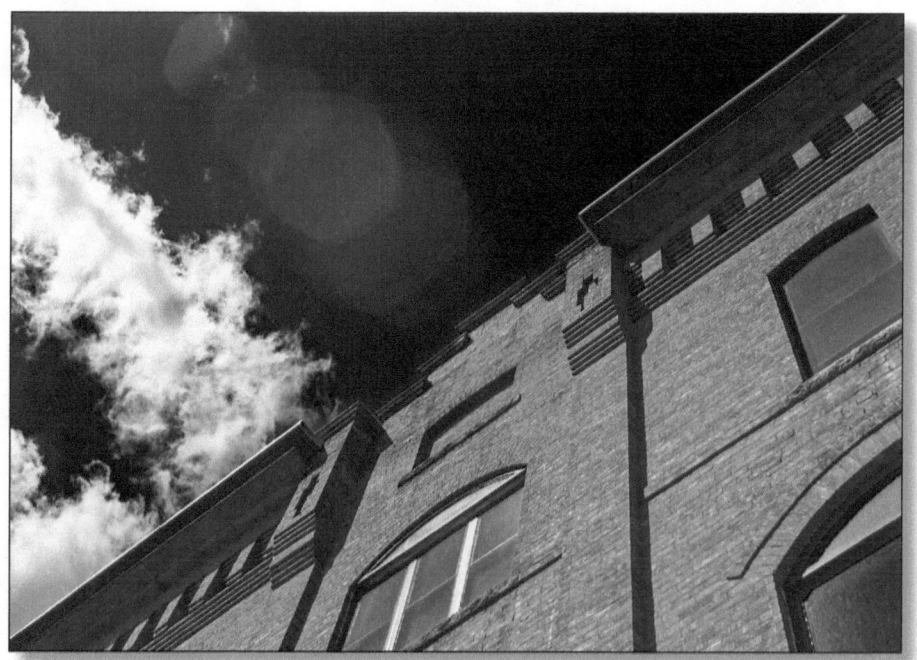

Ballston Spa, N.Y., April 12, 2014.
Canon EOS 10D, 30mm, f/5.6, 1/1000, ISO 200, P, pattern metering.
© 2014, 2015 by Shawn M. Tomlinson

people's photography, but it generally is the lowest quality lens from each manufacturer. It essentially is an enticement to buy the camera without forcing the consumer to have to then choose a lens. The truth is pros rarely use the kit lens, even if they are shooting with entry-level DSLRs. They usually replace them with better built, sharper lenses.

The better the lens, the better the image quality. To get the absolute best image from a 24-megapixel DSLR, you should use a prime, fixed-focal length 35mm lens or another prime lens such as a 50mm, 28mm or 24mm.

A zoom lens, as long as it is top quality, also will make use of the high resolution.

The kit lens won't.

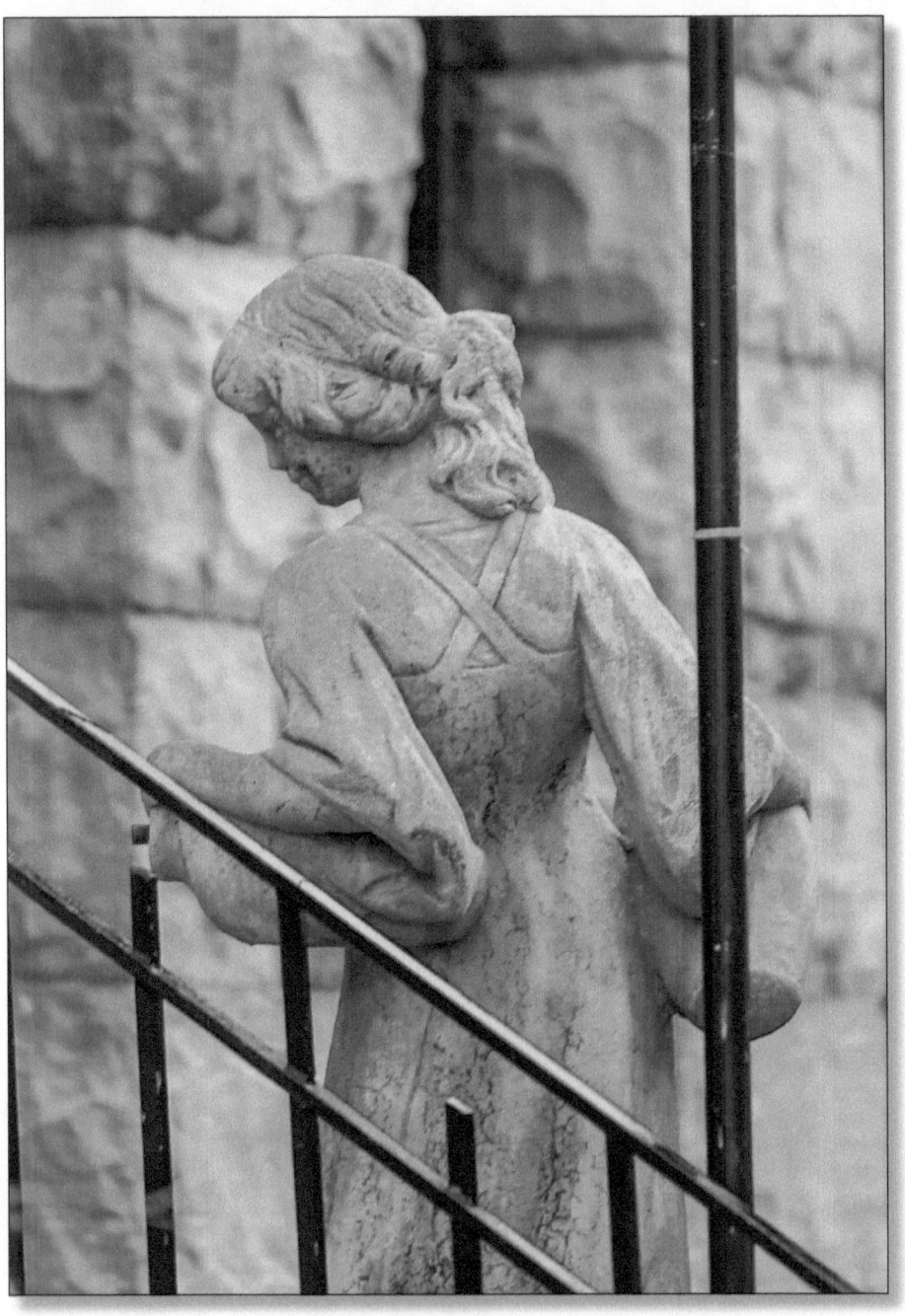

Saratoga Springs, N.Y., Nov. 30, 2013.
Pentax *ist DS, 200mm, f/5.6, 1/45, ISO 200, P, center-weighted metering.
© 2013, 2015 by Shawn M. Tomlinson

Part 4:
Choosing a Brand

I used to have a severe prejudice against one brand of camera largely because of my snooty upbringing by the photography magazines of the 1970s and 1980s. I had a sense of awe about two other brands, and chose the one I did based upon what I read and my purist sense of what a photographer was. Hey, I was a teenager. I bought into the marketing.

The truth is that of all the brands mentioned — well, unmentioned — above, three still make cameras, and all are good, solid pieces of equipment.

Only recently have I had the opportunity to work with the brand I irrationally hated and the one I was in

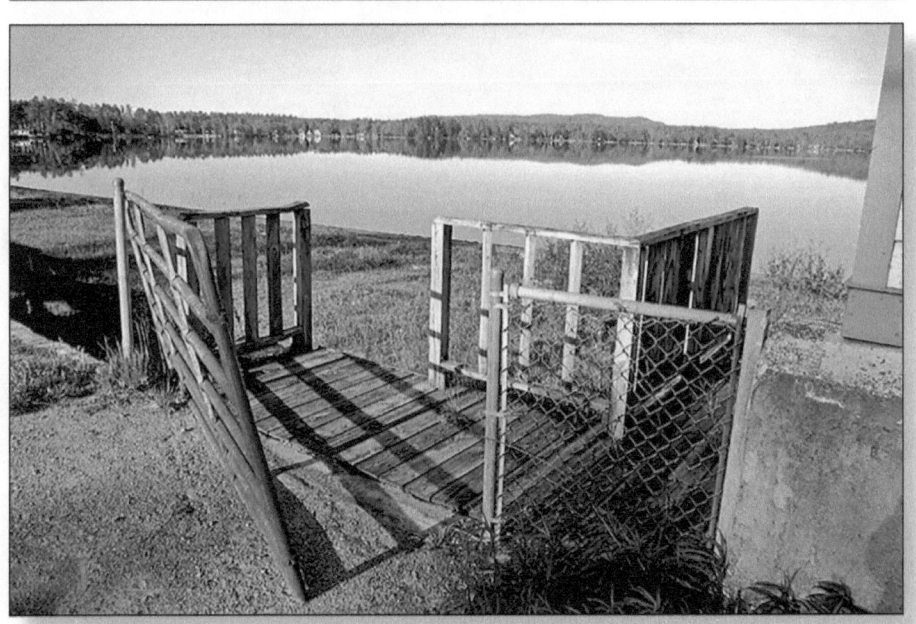

Caroga Lake, N.Y., May 18, 2012.
Pentax *ist DS, 18mm, f/8, 1/180, ISO 200 , P, center-weighted metering.
© 2012, 2015 by Shawn M. Tomlinson

awe of, and there are good and bad things about each.

Which camera you will like best really depends upon your eye as well as how the camera feels in your hand.

By eye, I mean what the images look like when you see them on a computer screen or in print. By the other, well, that's obvious.

It may not seem logical, but you will be much more likely to really get to know and love a camera that just *feels* right to you.

Not one of the major DSLR makers makes a bad camera. You really can't go wrong with any of these brands.

I'll give you my personal observations to help you along.

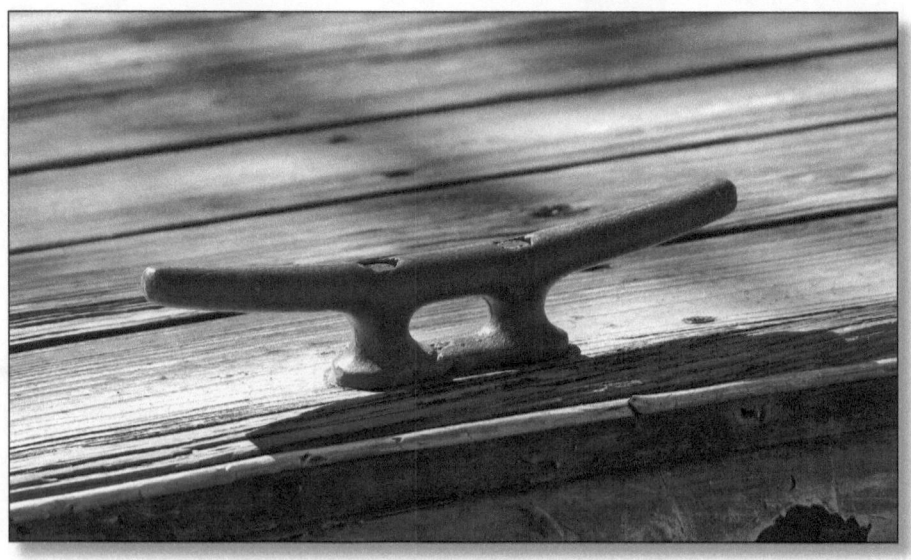

Boat Launch, Broadalbin, N.Y., Oct. 29, 2013.
Pentax *ist DS, 80mm, f/8, 1/250, ISO 200, P, center-weighted metering.
© 2013, 2015 by Shawn M. Tomlinson

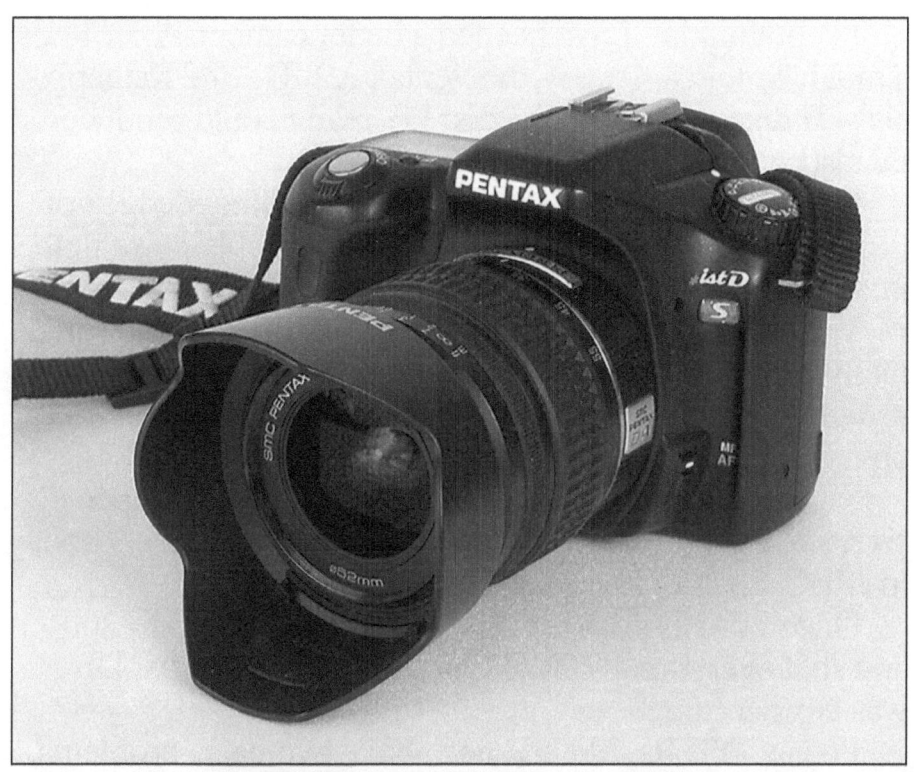

Photo: Rainer Knäpper, Free Art License (http://artlibre.org/licence/lal/en)

Pentax *ist DS

Pentax *ist DS (6.1 megapixels; $99).
Pentax made the first really good SLR film camera I owned, the fully manual Pentax MX.

I loved the camera and shot thousands of rolls of film through it. When it finally came time for an autofocus SLR film camera, I stuck with Pentax and bought a PZ-10.

When it became inevitable that I must move to digital, I bought Pentax's first consumer DSLR, the stupidly named *ist DS.

I loved it but hated it too because it produced really grainy images with lots of red-green-blue noise throughout.

I kept thinking I just needed a better camera. After I got a much better camera — the Pentax K20D, 14.2 megapixels — I discovered that the *ist DS really could produce fantastic photos.

It had been my own stupidity and my "knowledge" of film photography that produced all that terrible noise in the images.

With film, I usually shot at the highest film speed (originally called ASA and later called ISO) I could afford, usually 400 ASA/ISO. When I got the *ist DS, I cranked it up to 3200 ISO because it would go that far.

SD memory cards at that time also were very expensive, so to get the most out of my $90 1gb SanDisk, I shot in JPEG, another thing that caused noise.

Once I finally realized this, I changed the ISO to 200 and shot everything in RAW, and suddenly, the *ist DS was a *great* camera.

Pentax DSLRs, old and new, have two basic problems. They don't focus well in low light situations, and they make some colors pale, even when increasing the saturation in-camera.

On the plus side, they are very well built, better sealed against the weather than most lower-end cameras, and have a wide range of really good lenses.

Pentax DSLRs

Prior to the release of the Pentax *ist DS, the company released the semi-pro *ist D. Shortly after the DS, it released the cheaper *ist DL. Both the DS and DL had second versions, designated with a "2." All of these have the same resolution, 6.1 megapixels.

I recommend the *ist DS for several reasons:

1) It's the one I own and am familiar with.

2) The *ist D usually is more expensive and has a few problems the DS does not.

3) The DL was the cheapest of the line and did not have a pentaprism, but rather a pentamirror. This makes viewing a bit darker.

All of them will take great photos as long as you follow the Two ABSOLUTE Rules®:

ALWAYS shoot in RAW

ALWAYS shoot at the lowest ISO possible.

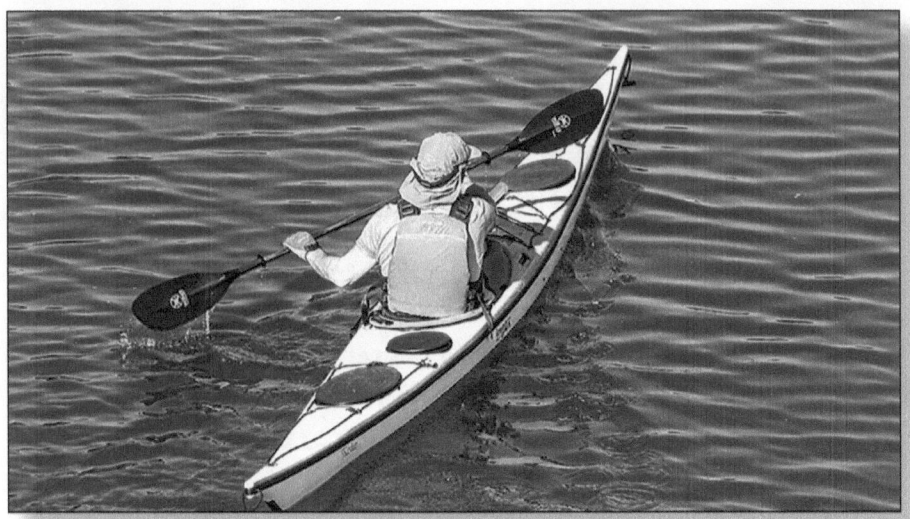

These are two photos I shot with the Pentax *ist DS.

The top image was shot from a bridge overlooking the Hudson River with a Pentax smc F 80-200mm f/4.7-5.6 lens with a shutter speed of 1/350 sec, at f/8 with ISO set at the minimum, 200.

Below, the brilliant colors of fall, here converted to black and white, were shot with the same lens at 1/180 sec; f/5.6; ISO 200, P, center-weighted metering.

Photos © 2014 by Shawn M. Tomlinson

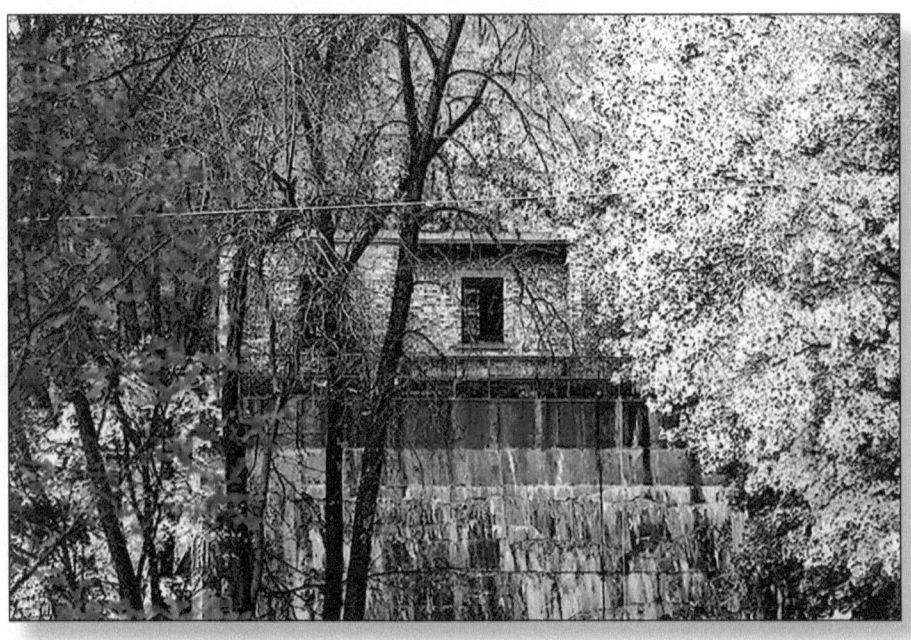

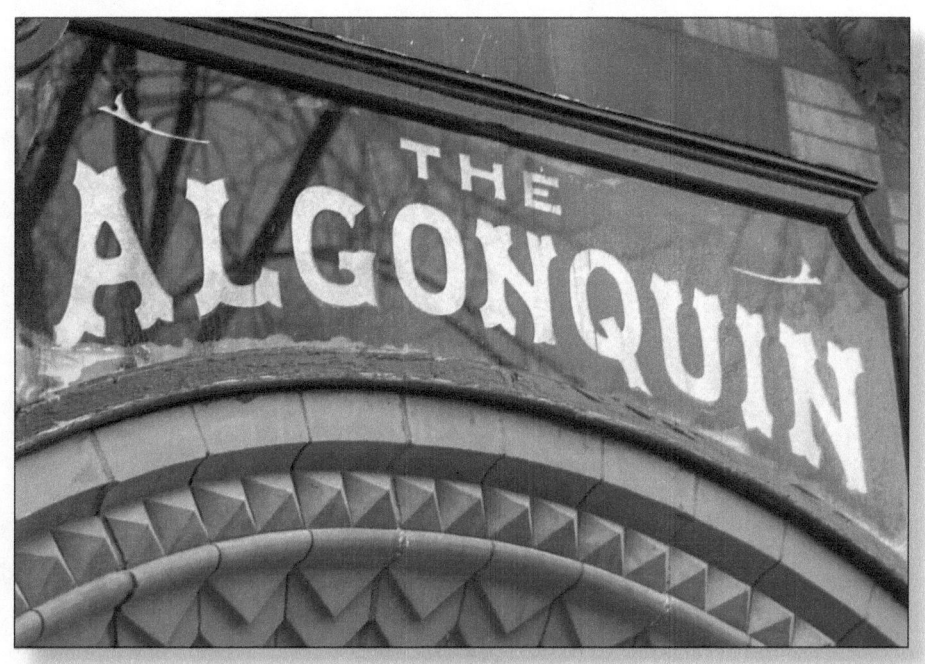

Above: Saratoga Springs, N.Y., Nov. 30, 2013.
Pentax *ist DS, 80mm, f/4.5, 1/90, ISO 200, P, center-weighted metering.

Below: Greenwich, N.Y., Nov. 36, 2013.
Pentax *ist DS, 135mm, f/4.5, 1/180, ISO 200, P, center-weighted metering.

© 2013, 2015 by Shawn M. Tomlinson

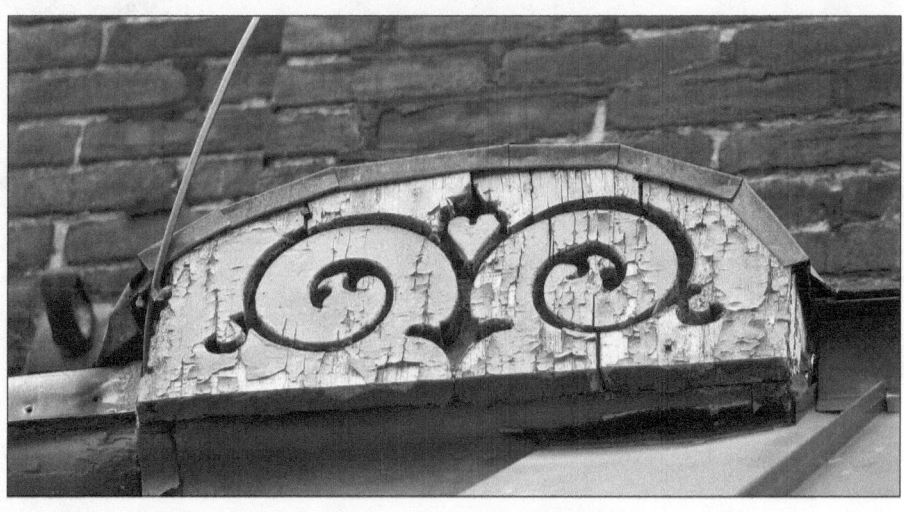

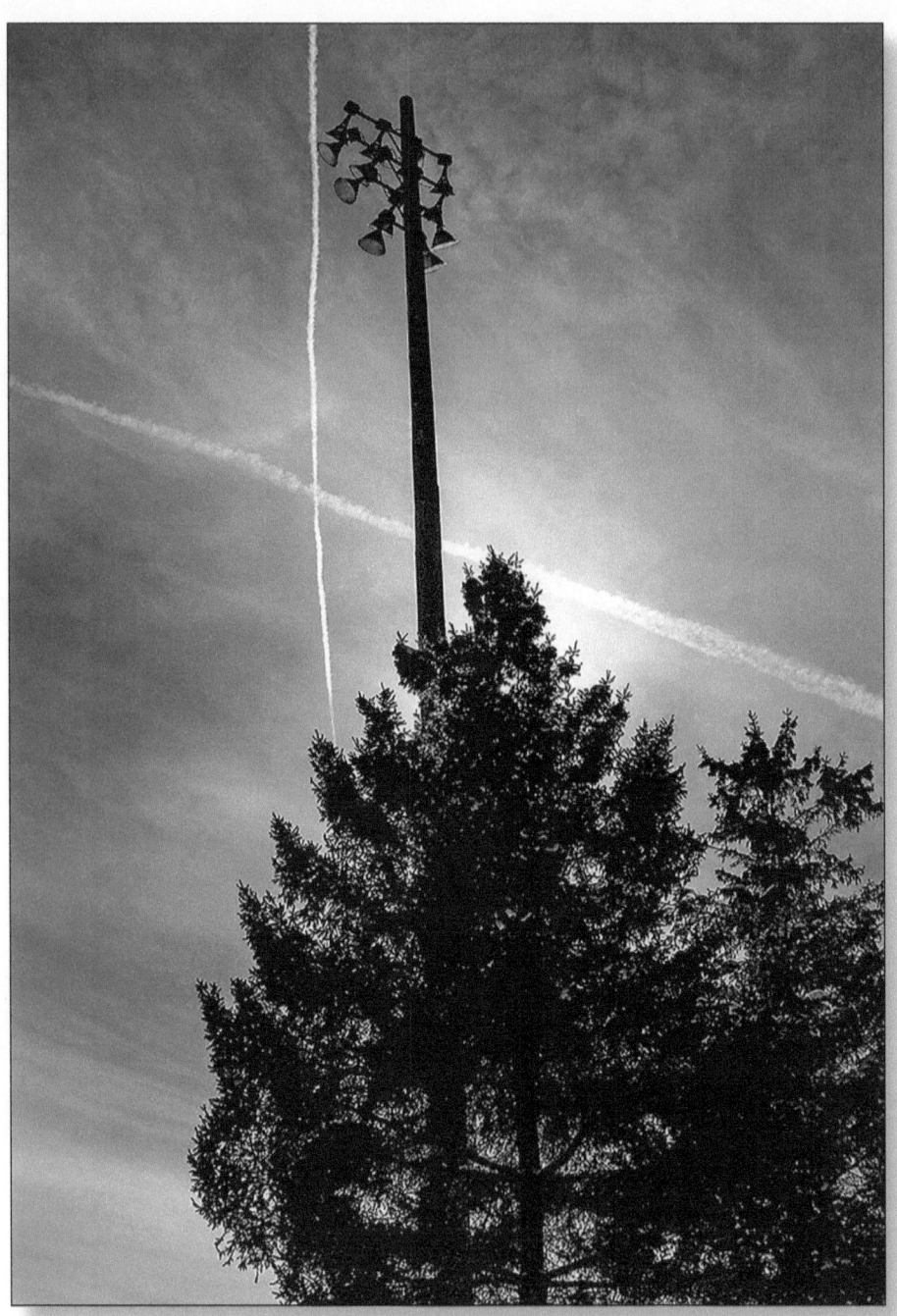

Saratoga Springs, N.Y., Feb. 8, 2014.
Nikon D70, 28mm, f/13, 1/640, ISO 200, P, pattern metering.
© 2014, 2015 by Shawn M. Tomlinson

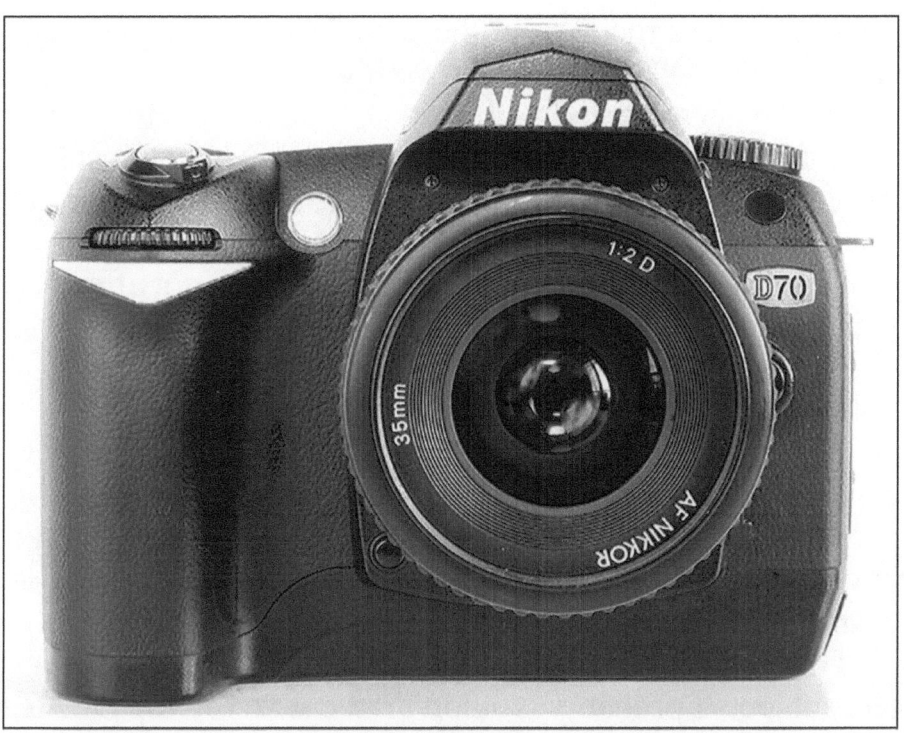

Photo: © *Marie-Lan Nguyen / Wikimedia Commons*

Nikon D70

Nikon D70 (6.1 megapixels; $69).

Finally, I got to own and shoot with a Nikon.

I'd always wanted one, of course, and had been buying up very cheap unwanted Nikon film cameras for a while, but when I saw I could get a Nikon DSLR for $69, well, I couldn't wait.

And I loved it immediately. It had better color rendition to my eye than my Pentax DSLRs, and it could focus in low-light conditions they could not.

I suddenly could take images in twilight or indoors of my black cat or of the moon and see detail, even hand-held. And it had that great, venerable name "Nikon" on it.

On the positive side, the D70 works with virtually every Nikkor lens made from the early 1970s through today. Only the non-AI early lenses won't work.

On the negative, it does have a significant lag time if you shoot fast. This means it takes time for the D70 to transfer images from its buffer to the memory card, and prevents you from shooting images while it does it.

Shooting like a normal person, this should not affect you.

If you shoot a lot of images fast like I do, it can be frustrating.

The great thing about the Nikon D70 and the other cameras recommended here is that because they are inexpensive, I feel like I can just grab one and go shoot. I don't have that worry at the back of my mind about damaging or destroying a very expensive DSLR.

This has made me shoot a lot more, and a lot more often, subjects I probably wouldn't have with my top DSLR.

These consumer-level cameras are not built tough like the pro-level ones, but take a little care, and they will handle well and for quite a while.

If you want rock-solid DSLRs — and there is a lot to be said in their favor — the budget breaks and the prices goes up significantly.

Nikon DSLRs

The first DSLR I ever used was the Nikon D1 pro camera at the newspaper where I was an editor. It won me immediately, but the $6,000 price tag back in 2002 was not remotely in my range.

By then, Nikon had released the D100, the D70 and the D80. I shot a lot with the newspaper's D80 until I bought my own DSLR. It was a great camera.

The D70, geared more toward the lower end — the retro equivalent of the Nikon D3300 — was calling me when I saw how cheap it was used.

Using the D70 every day proved to me why Nikon generally is considered the top DSLR maker, as it was the top SLR maker. It is a great, fairly solid, lightweight camera that I want to carry everywhere with me.

You will, too.

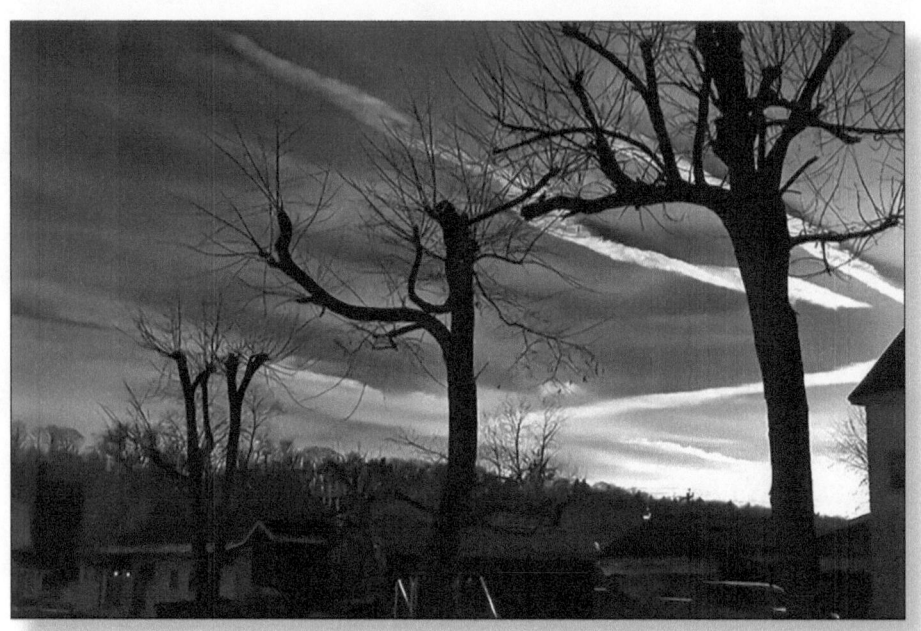

Above: Amsterdam, N.Y., March 9, 2014.
Nikon D70, 28mm, f/13, 1/640, ISO 250, P, pattern metering.

Below: Perth, N.Y., March 5, 2014.
Nikon D70, 70mm, f/13, 1/640, ISO 320, P, pattern metering.

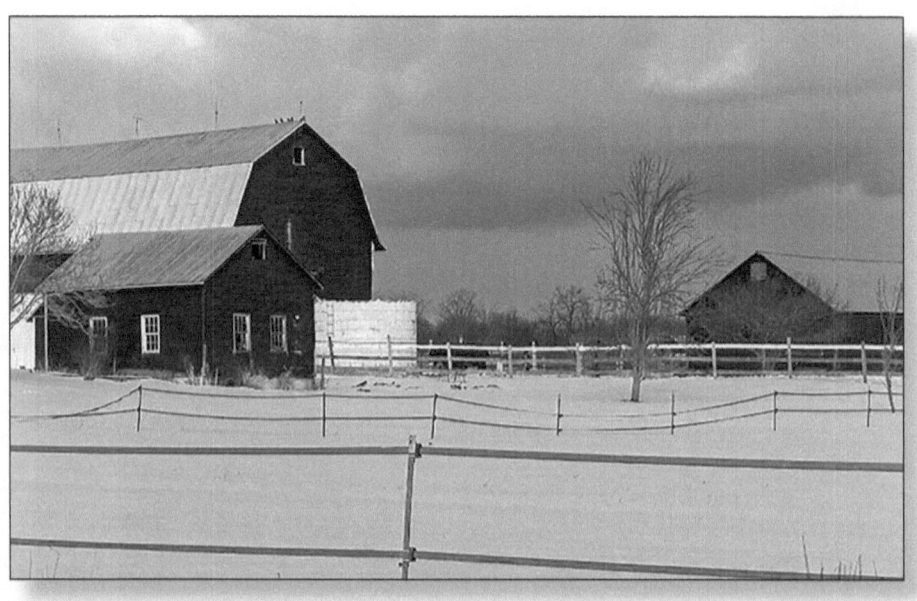

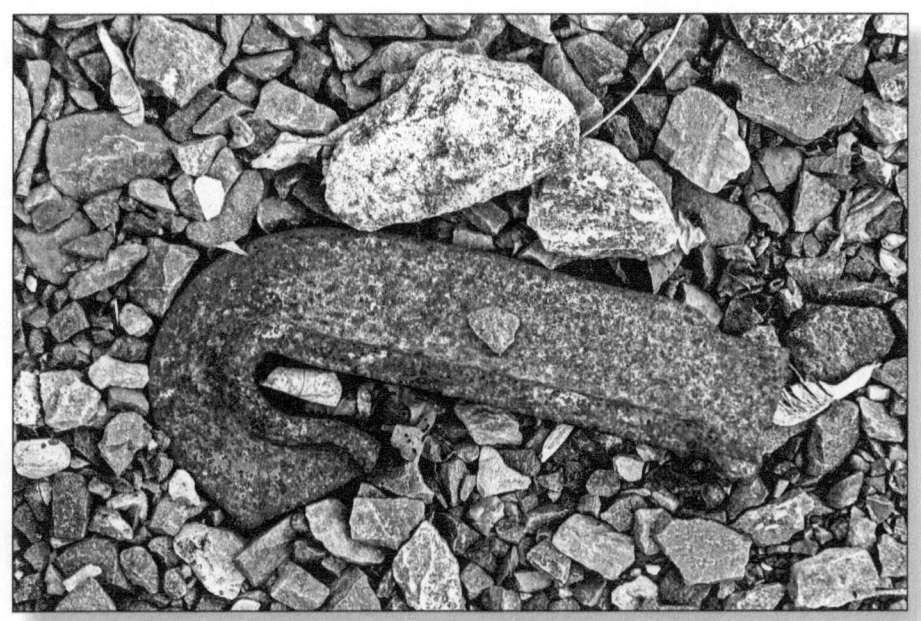

Above: Glenville, N.Y., April 14, 2014.
Nikon D70, 82mm, f/7.1, 1/200, ISO 200, P, pattern metering.

Below: Glenville, N.Y., April 14, 2014.
Nikon D70, 28mm, f/11, 1/500, ISO 200, P, pattern metering.

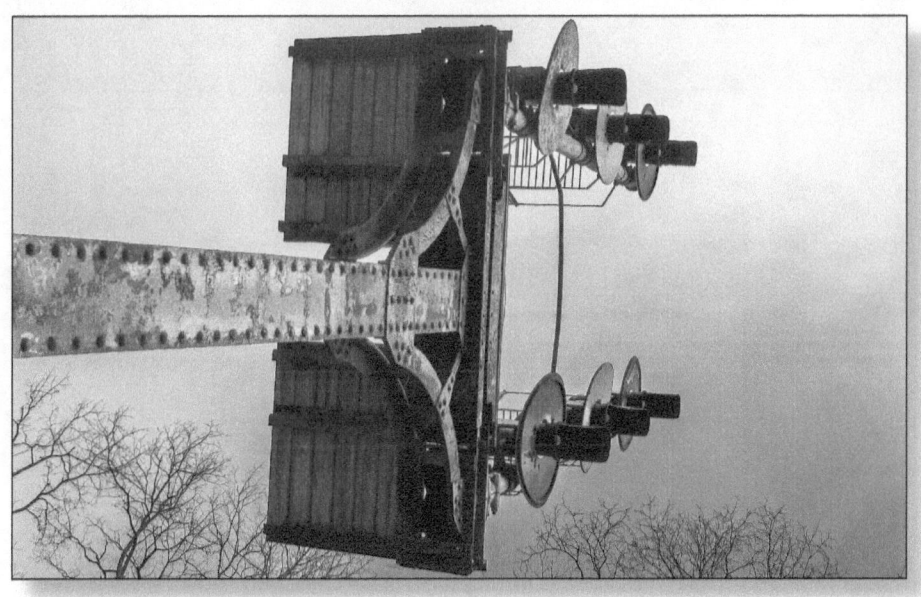

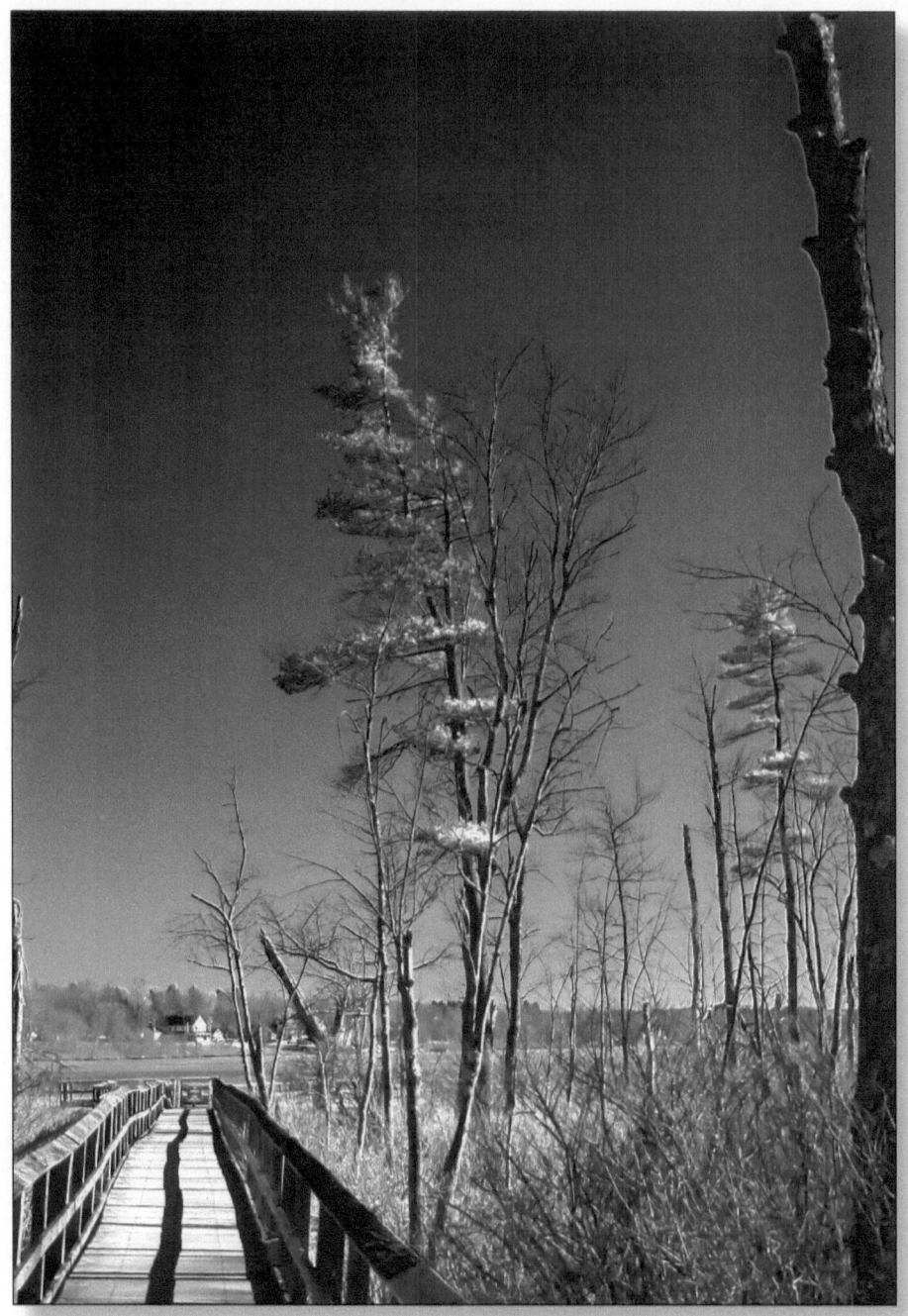

The lake, Ballston Lake, N.Y., April 6, 2014.
Canon EOS 10D, 28mm, f/6.7, 1/1000, ISO 200, M, pattern metering.
© 2014, 2015 by Shawn M. Tomlinson

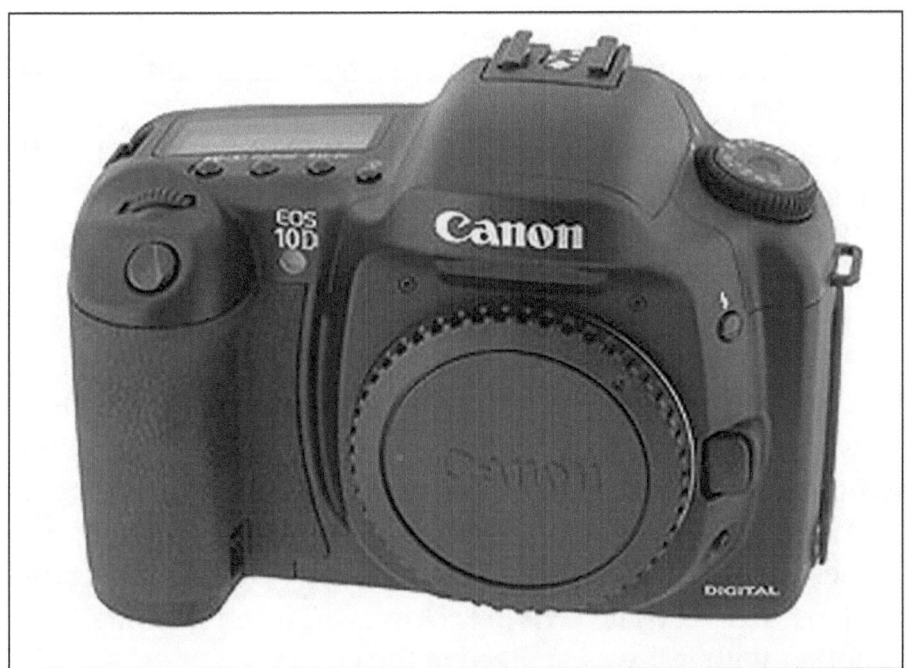

Canon EOS 10D

Canon EOS 10D (6.1 megapixels; $69).

OK, this is the brand I always hated and thought of as cheap and only for rubes. This opinion was based upon the film SLR the Canon AE-1 Program camera.

Then I bought a Canon A-1, then an AE-1, then, alas, the AE-1 Program, and realized that these really were great cameras, especially the A-1.

So, when I saw the Canon EOS 10D DSLR for $69 that included the pretentious yet useful battery grip, well, what the hell, I bought it.

And it made me a convert.

The color right out of the camera is superior in my opinion to the Pentax *ist DS, the Nikon D70 and even, sadly, my Pentax K20D.

On the down side, the Canon EOS 10D has the slowest startup time of any of these cameras, from cold start or from sleep. That can be frustrating.

Also, like the D70, it can produce a significant lag time if you shoot fast.

The Canon EOS 10D, though, was my go-to DSLR for shooting every day for some time. The lens I use, a Canon EF II 28-80mm f/3.5-5.6, is faster and more accurate focusing than the Nikon D70. It also doesn't have slippage or lens creep, a phenomenon that can occur in older lenses that slowly changes the focal length through gravity if you hold it wrong. The Nikkor lens has this problem.

I admit that the Canon EOS 10D felt plasticy and crappy to me when it first arrived and I could only stare at it because the lens was very late arriving. However, when I did start shooting with it, I was amazed at the color.

To be honest, this cheap, old DSLR has made me a convert to Canon. My next high end DSLR was the full-frame Canon EOS 1Ds.

Since the original appearance of this volume as an eBook, I have used the Canon EOS 20D instead of the 10D because the latter died a month after I started shooting with it. That says nothing bad about the 10D. I just got one that was about to die. It happens with older, used DSLRs. KEH, from whom I bought it refunded it immediately.

I bring this up for a couple of reasons. The color on the 10D was marginally better than the 20D. I have shot with both — borrowing a 10D from a friend — and still find that, straight from the camera, the 10D has a bit better color.

That said, though, the 20D is a superior camera and the prices have come down a bit, letting you get one for around $100.

The main advantages of the 20D over the 10D include

the speed with which you can shoot with it and the fact that you can use the cheaper, newer EF-S lenses with it. There is virtually no lag time starting up and the 20D shoots at 5 frames per second. That speed is comparable to many modern DSLRs and superior to many entry-level models.

Either DSLR will give you great images with that warm, vivid Canon color. Either would be a great starter DSLR.

If I went back in time and told my 16-year-old self this, he'd scowl at me and never believe me.

Canon DSLRs

Canon got into or perhaps created the mid-level consumer DSLR market with the D30 3.2 megapixel DSLR, then moved to the D60. The company made some major, radical changes and came out with the 10D. It is the predecessor to all that followed in that line: The 20D, 30D, 40D and 50D. The 60D and 70D are departures from that line despite the names.

The one drawback you might have if you acquire a Canon EOS 10D is that it cannot use modern Canon EF-S lenses. This prevents you from getting really wide angle shots on the cropped sensor. However, it means that all the autofocus EF lenses do work, and older versions of these can be cheap.

Also note that, unlike Nikon and Pentax, Canon changed its lens mount when it went to autofocus cameras. No manual focus Canon FD will work on an EOS film or digital camera without an adapter.

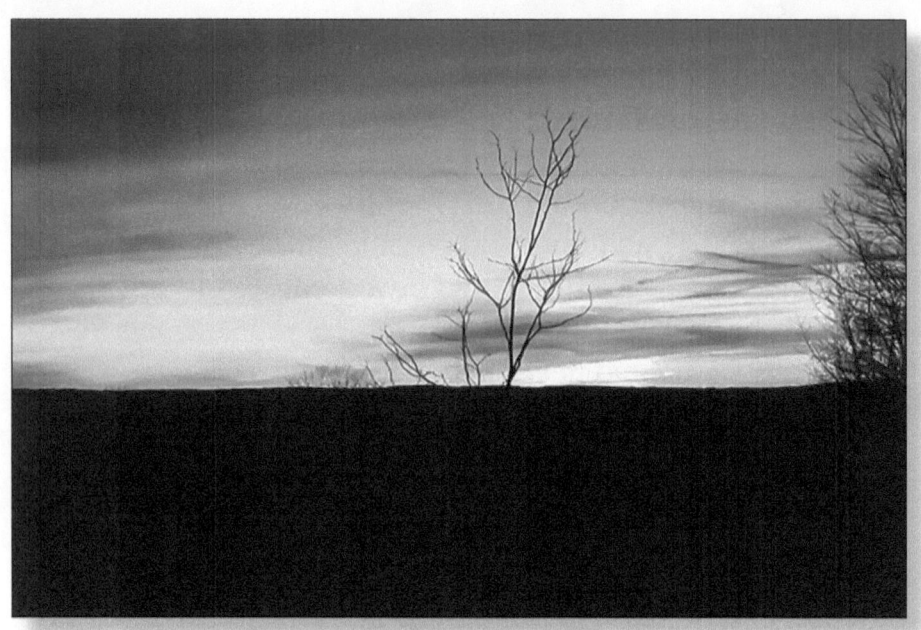

Above: Amsterdam, N.Y., March 16, 2014.
Canon EOS 10D, 70mm, f/5.6, 1/180, ISO 1600, P, pattern metering.

Below: Ballston Lake, N.Y., March 12, 2014.
Canon EOS 10D, 80mm, f/6.7, 1/180, ISO 400, P, pattern metering.

© 2014, 2015 by Shawn M. Tomlinson

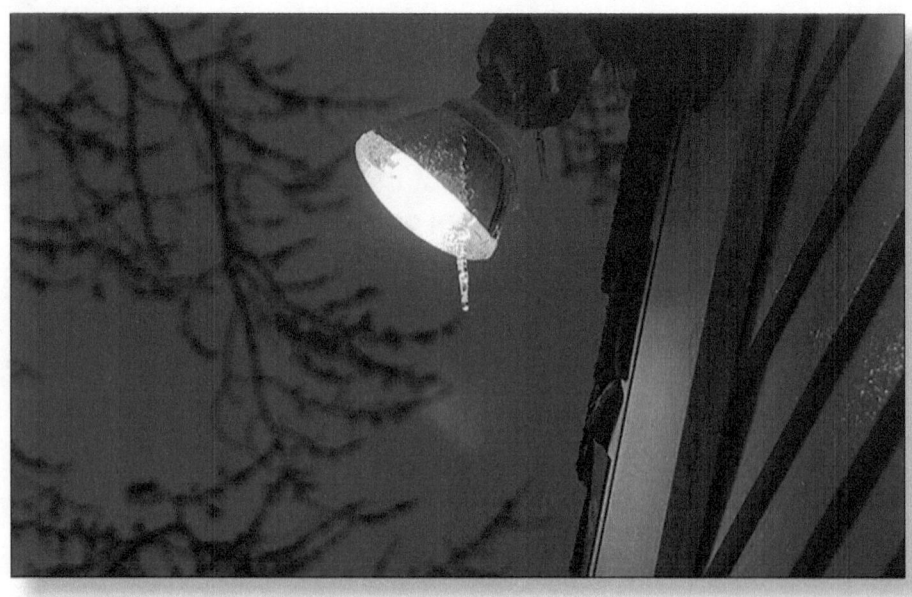

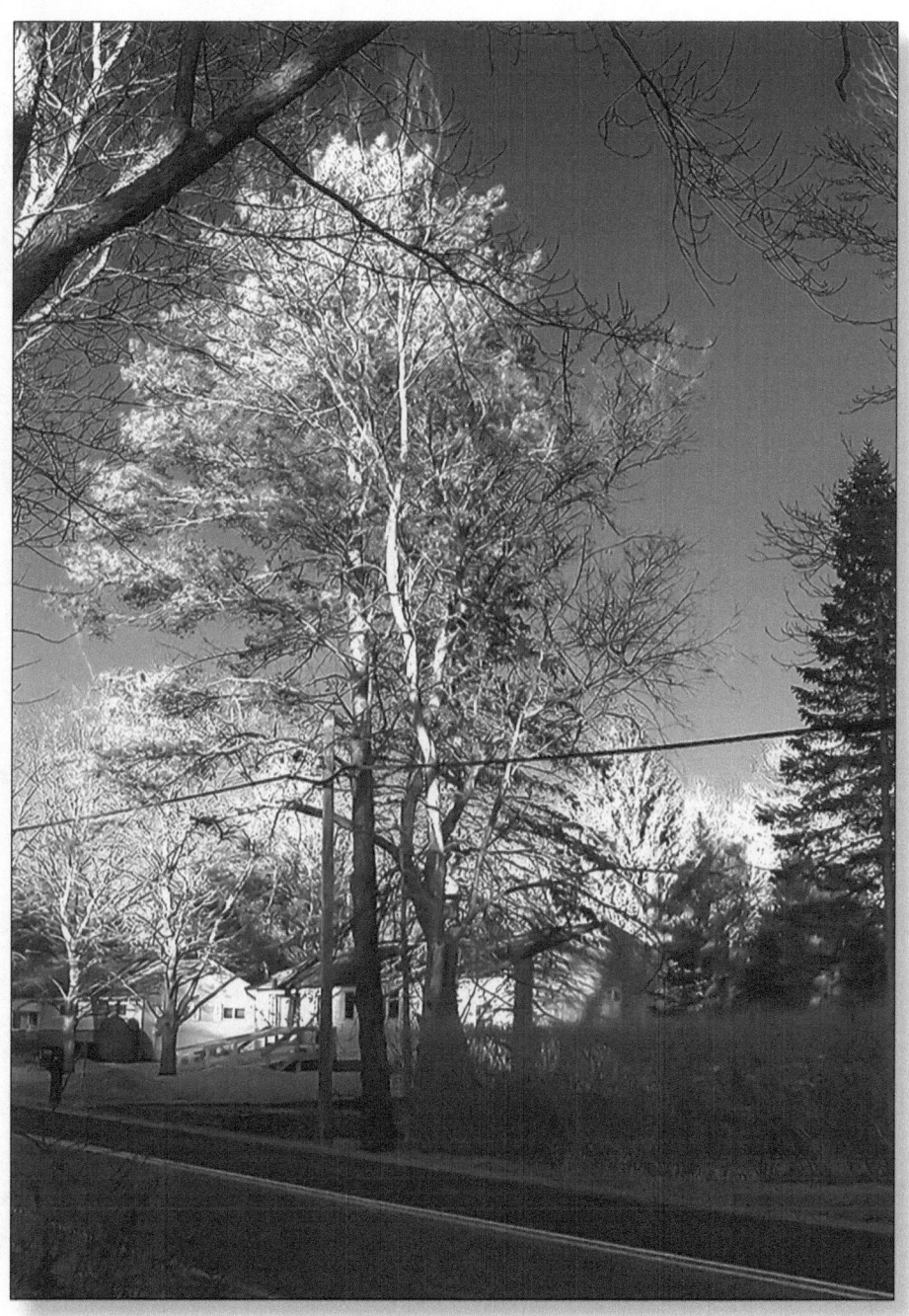

Ballston Lake, N.Y., March 17, 2014.
Nikon D70, 28mm, f/7.1, 1/200, ISO 200, P, pattern metering.
© 2014, 2015 by Shawn M. Tomlinson

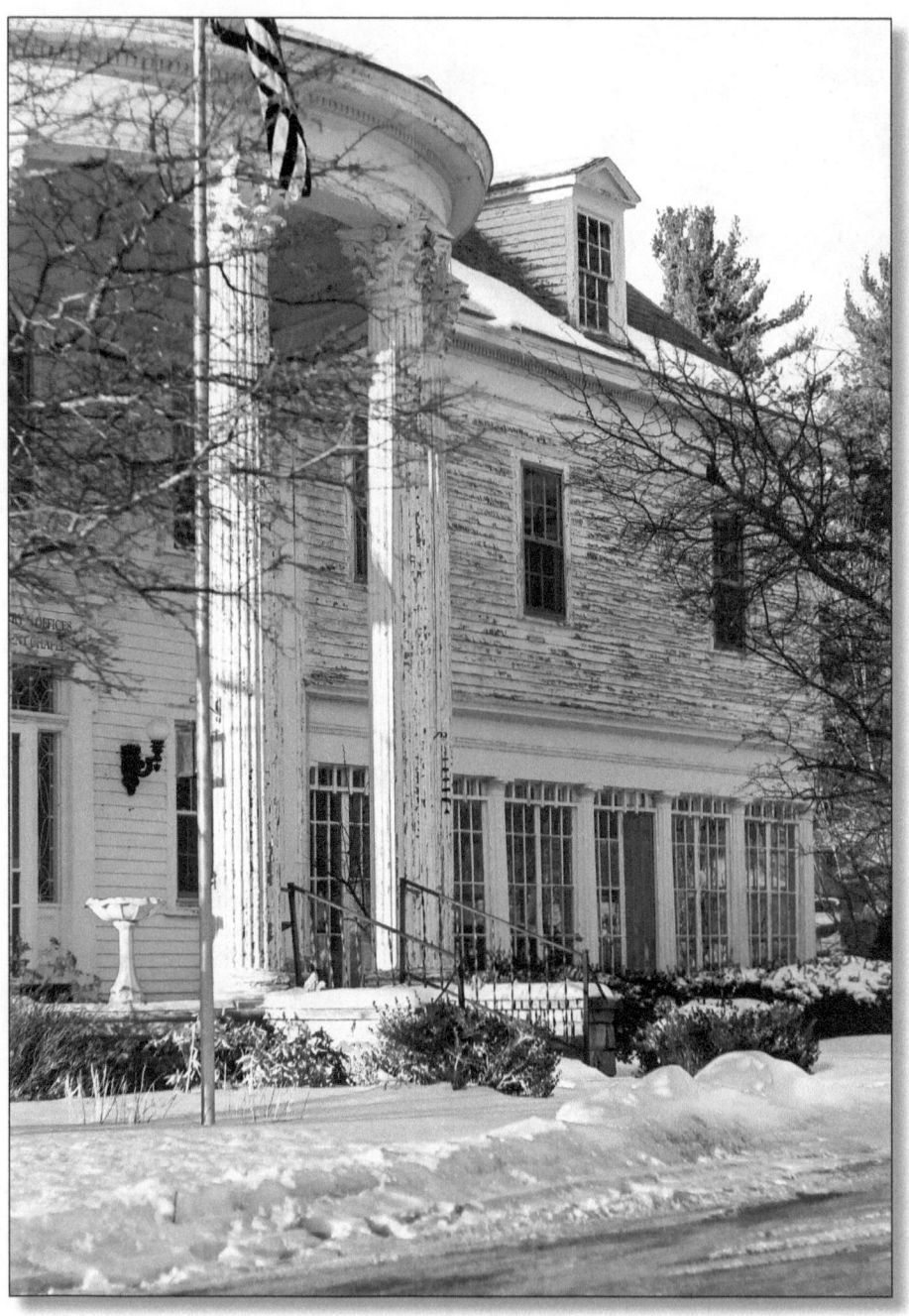

Robert W. Chambers' Broadalbin House, Broadalbin, N.Y., Jan. 23, 2015.
Sony A100, 50mm, f/2.5, 1/4000, ISO 200, Tv, pattern metering.
© 2015 by Shawn M. Tomlinson

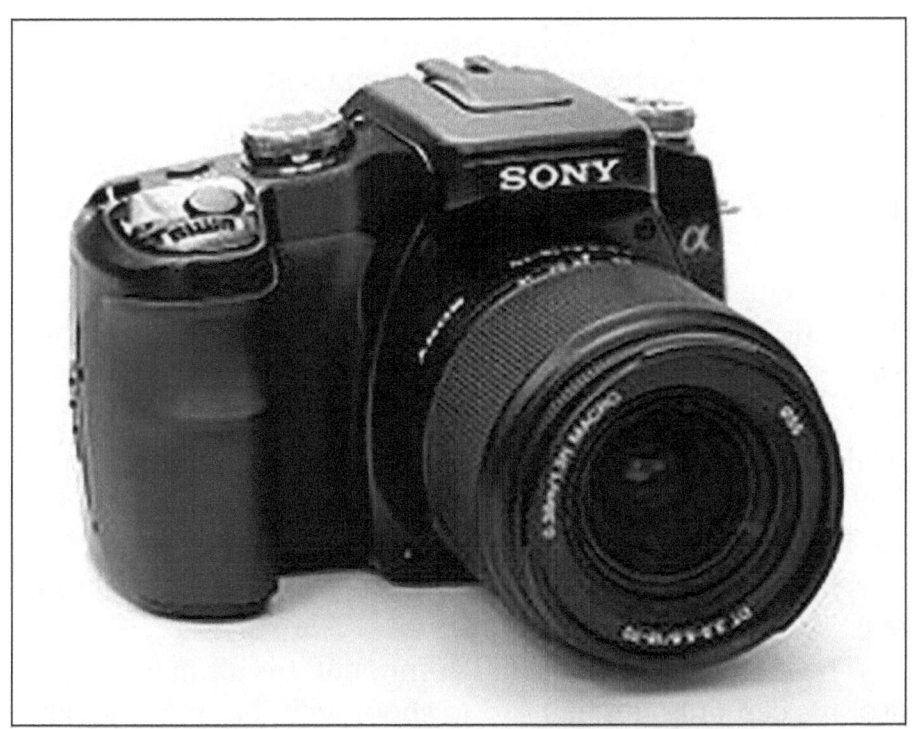

Wikipedia

Sony A100

Sony A100 (10.2 megapixels; $115).

In the first edition of this book, I wrote "Admittedly, as of this writing, I have yet to get my hands on my first Sony DSLR, but since I already own a 75-300mm Minolta autofocus zoom lens, I will be getting one soon."

Since that edition, I did buy a Sony A100

The reason? The sharpness.

Again, the original text: "In samples I have seen from reputable test organizations, the A100 has the sharpest images of any of these cameras. The color is a little paler, like the Pentax, but the sharpness is greater than the others. This may be an unfair comparison because the Sony A100 is a newer camera with better resolution, but it appears sharper even than my K20D and its 14.2 megapixels."

I quote all this because now having used the A100 for some time, I can say that images are very sharp, but also that the samples I saw previously did not do the color justice. I have found that the color from the A100 is fantastic.

Two things contribute to the sharpness. I'm using, almost exclusively, a Minolta Maxxum 50mm f/1.7 lens on the A100, and the A100 has Sony's stupidly named Super Steady Shot technology. The former is a very sharp prime lens. The latter, silly as the name is, actually works very well. I've shot at relatively slow shutter speeds with a 75-300mm lens on the camera and have yet to see lens blur.

That means a lot, especially if you shoot with longer telephoto lenses, but even helps in low light with the 50mm lens.

The A100 is a bit clunky, I admit, but it is a fun camera to use. It's certainly not that fast to shoot with, but it is a great starter DSLR. I even wrote an eBook specifically about the joys of this camera. (*Shawn M. Tomlinson's Guide to Photography Vol. 10: Great Starter DSLR: Revisiting the Sony A100*).

It typically costs a little more than the other DSLRs mentioned here, but it also has slightly higher resolution. Where the real savings will come in is with lenses. Because it takes Minolta Maxxum lenses, you can get great glass for less money than virtually any of the other brands.

For example, a standard prime fixed-focal-length 50mm lens from Canon or Nikon on the used market costs around $100. For Pentax, around $170. I bought that Minolta Maxxum 50mm f/1.7 — which is slightly faster (lets in more light) than the others — for $45.

For a bit more money than the A100, you can get the Sony A230, which has some improvements. Among these and a big selling point to me is two memory card slots. This is a trend now in higher-end DSLRs and provides either backup or double the storage capacity. I use the two slots on my Nikon D7000 daily, so it is very useful. The one drawback is that the second slot is for Sony's own Memory Stick Pro Duo memory cards.

The Sony A100, like the Canon EOS 10D (or 20D), the Nikon D70 and the Pentax *ist DS, produces fantastic images. It also is easy to learn and use. And, really, just a lot of fun to use.

Sony DSLRs

Sony has been all over the place with its cameras and now seems to be concentrating on mirrorless models.

I never really considered Sony DSLRs until I saw the image quality in a variety of samples. An added bonus for me was that I already owned a 75-300mm Minolta Maxxum-mount autofocus lens that works on Sony DSLRs. This is true because Sony bought the now-defunct Konica-Minolta camera technology.

This is a bonus for you, too, because even really good Minolta Maxxum lenses are cheap used.

Sony has worked hard to compete with virtually every other brand and level of beginner, enthusiast, semi-pro and pro camera. It has had some success with this, and, especially in mirrorless cameras and video, has excelled.

It all started with Sony bought the camera technology from Minolta as it was dying. The A100 was Sony's first DSLR with that technology.

Put a prime 50mm f/1.7 lens on the A100, and you've got a brilliant camera with brilliant images.

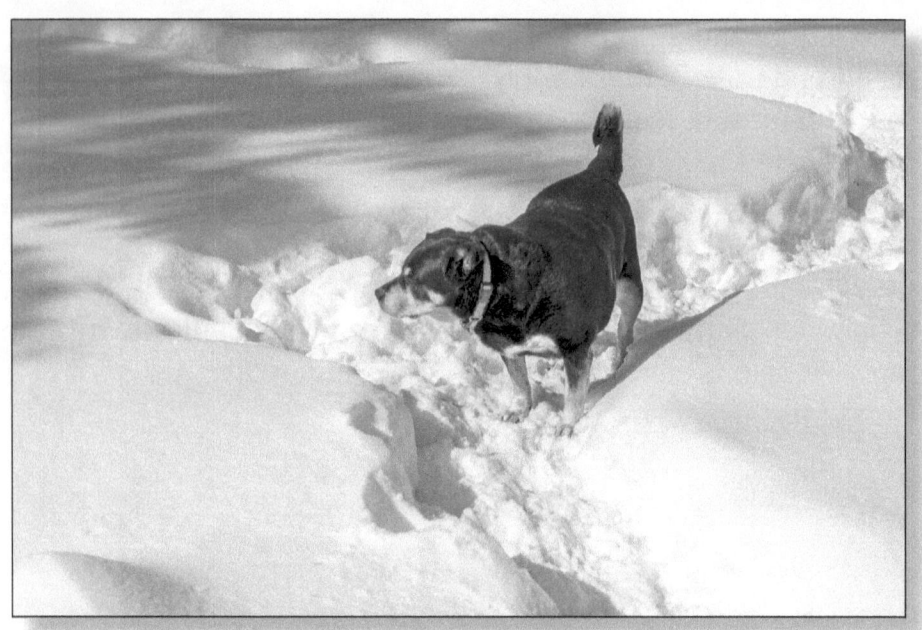

Above: Baby, Ballston Lake, N.Y., Feb. 23, 2015.
Sony A100, 50mm, f/3.2, 1/4000, ISO 200, Tv, pattern metering.

Below: Saratoga Springs, N.Y., Jan. 10, 2015.
Sony A100, 300mm, f/8, 1/4000, ISO 100, Tv, pattern metering.

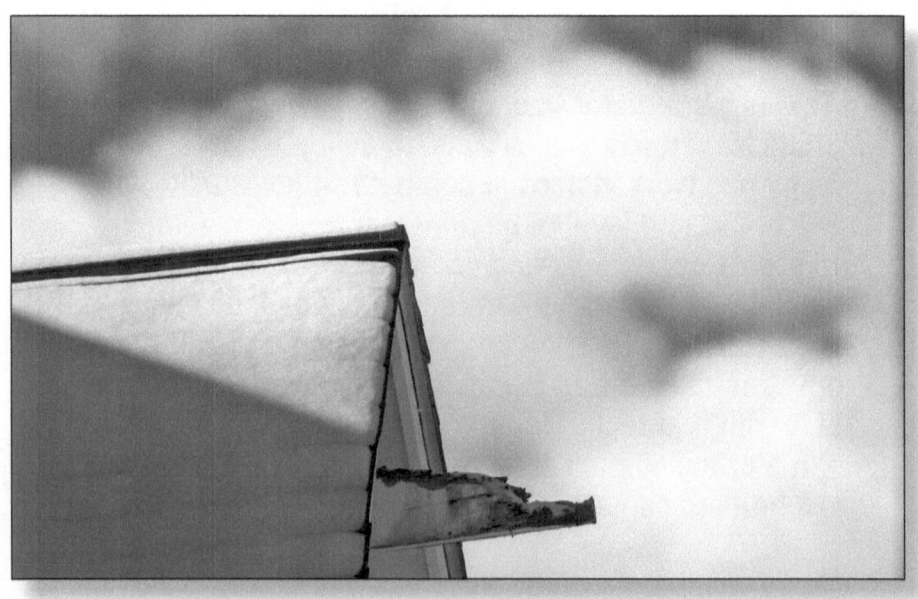

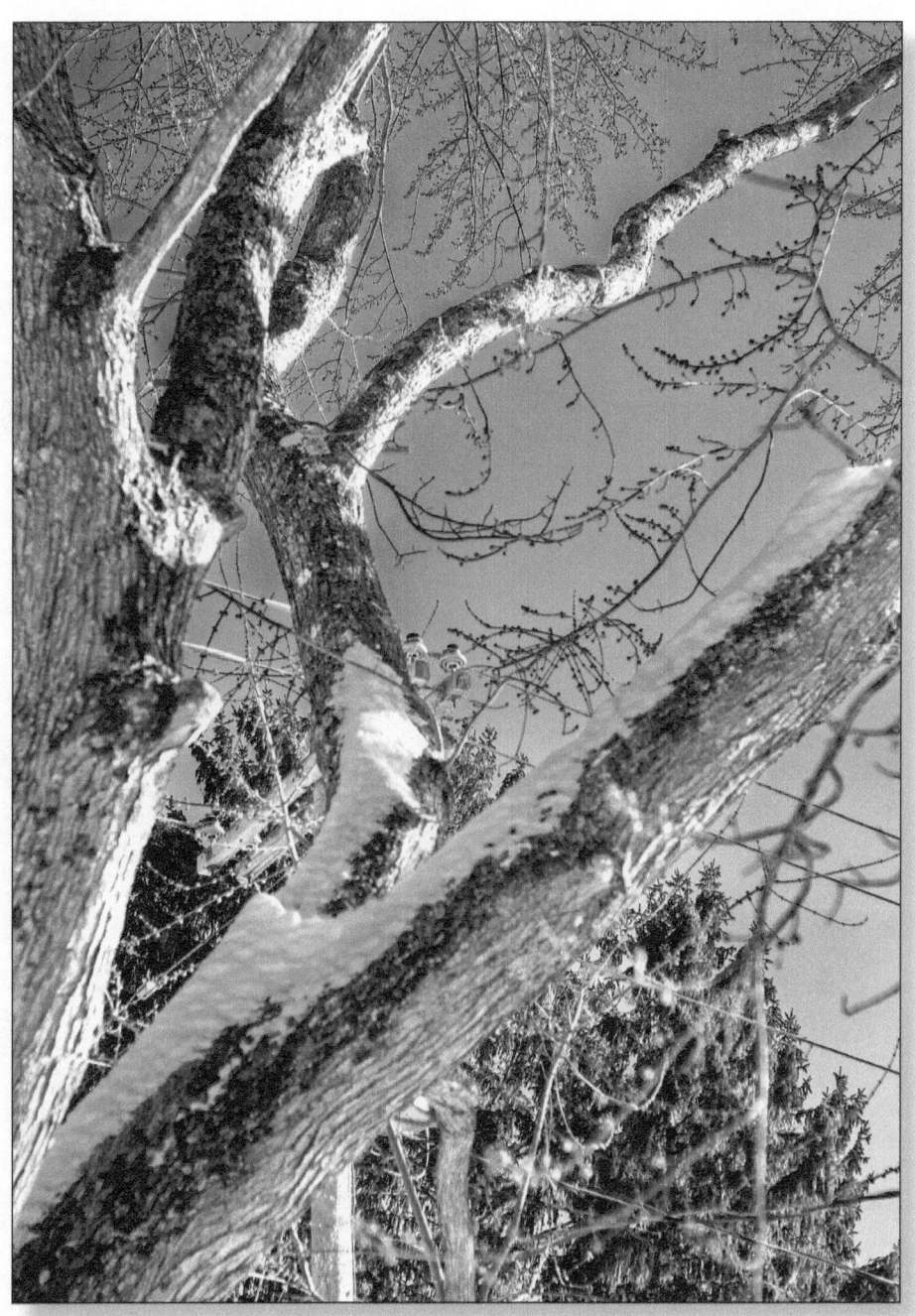

Ballston Lake, N.Y., Feb. 23, 2015.
Sony A100, 50mm, f/3.5, 1/2500, ISO 100, Tv, pattern metering.
© 2015 by Shawn M. Tomlinson

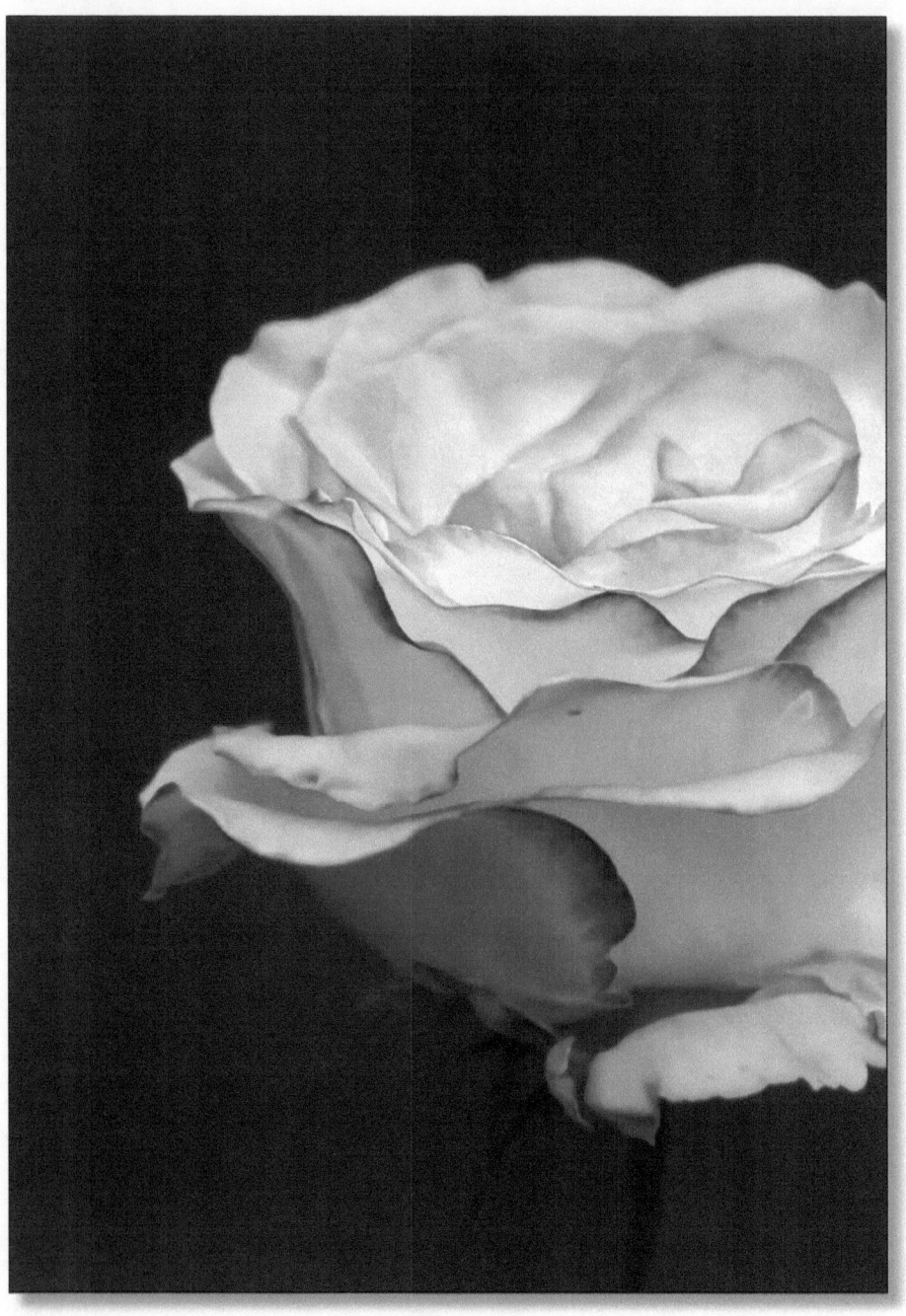

Central Park, Schenectady, N.Y., Aug. 17, 2014.
Nikon D70, 300mm, f/6, 1/1000, ISO 400, Tv, pattern metering.
© 2015 by Shawn M. Tomlinson

Part 4:
Choosing a Brand

A few years ago, each of these cameras cost hundreds or thousands of dollars, yet you can get each of them for less than $110. For that money, you also get a battery and appropriate charger, if you buy from my favorite used photographic equipment dealer, KEH. com. No, I don't get a commission from this company to promote it, and I don't even get a discount. I just like the company. They are overly cautious with their condition grading system, meaning if you buy something KEH marks as BGN (bargain) it probably will look and feel closer to new than you expect. Once in a while you might get a better price by bidding on eBay, but you never know really the condition or even if a camera works from there.

The other two major used camera dealers are Adorama and B&H. I have not had good luck with these companies. I had to threaten to go to the New York State Attorney General to get a refund from Adorama for a Nikon D2x they sent me that never worked.

KEH always has been a great dealer for me. They deal with returns quickly when necessary, but in general sell great cameras and lenses. And the prices are the best around.

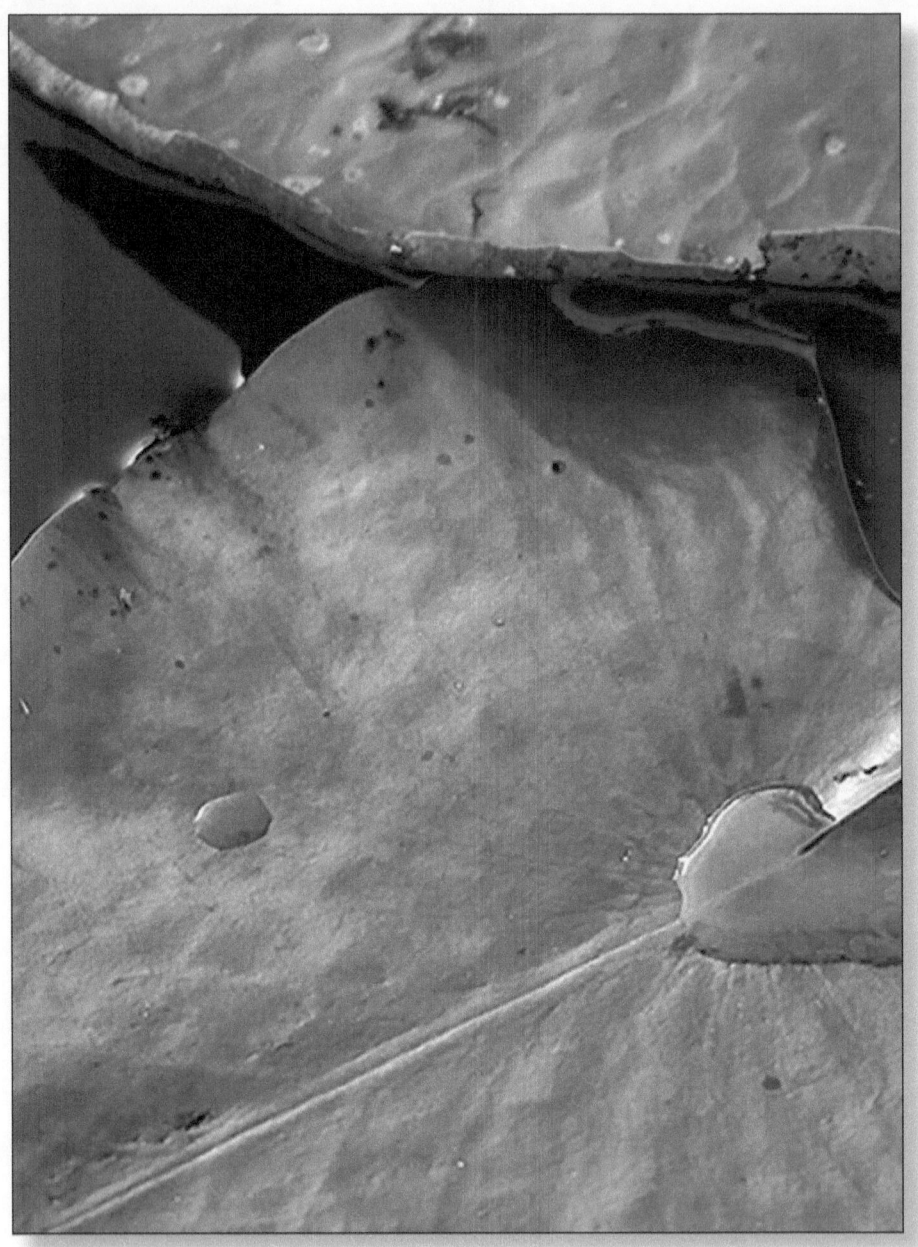

This closeup shows the fine detail possible even on a 6.1 megapixel DSLR. I shot this with the Pentax *ist DS, 200mm, 1/90, f/5.6; ISO 200, P, pattern metering.

Part 5

Choosing a Lens

This is where, if you know what to look for, you often can save a lot of money, even for good lenses.

In case I haven't said it enough yet: Lenses are the most important part of photography.

The better the glass, the better the images. Period.

Price does not always dictate quality, however, and some really expensive lenses are no better or even not as good as much cheaper ones.

Both Canon and Pentax have specific designations — other than just high price tags — for their high-end professional lenses. For Canon, it is "L." If you see an "L" in the name, it is a top-quality Canon lens. Each "L" lens also has a red band around the front of the lens.

For Pentax there are two: "DA*" and "Limited." All current Pentax digital lenses are "DA," but when you see that asterisk attached, it's a better grade lens. "Limited," also with a red band, is the current top-of-the-line Pentax glass.

Can you buy any of these and keep within our budget? Absolutely not.

These lenses are what to strive for if you decide serious photography really means something to you.

For our budget, we want to get the best lens for the least amount of money.

The best way to do this is to not buy "digital" or crop-sensor lenses, but rather older film lenses.

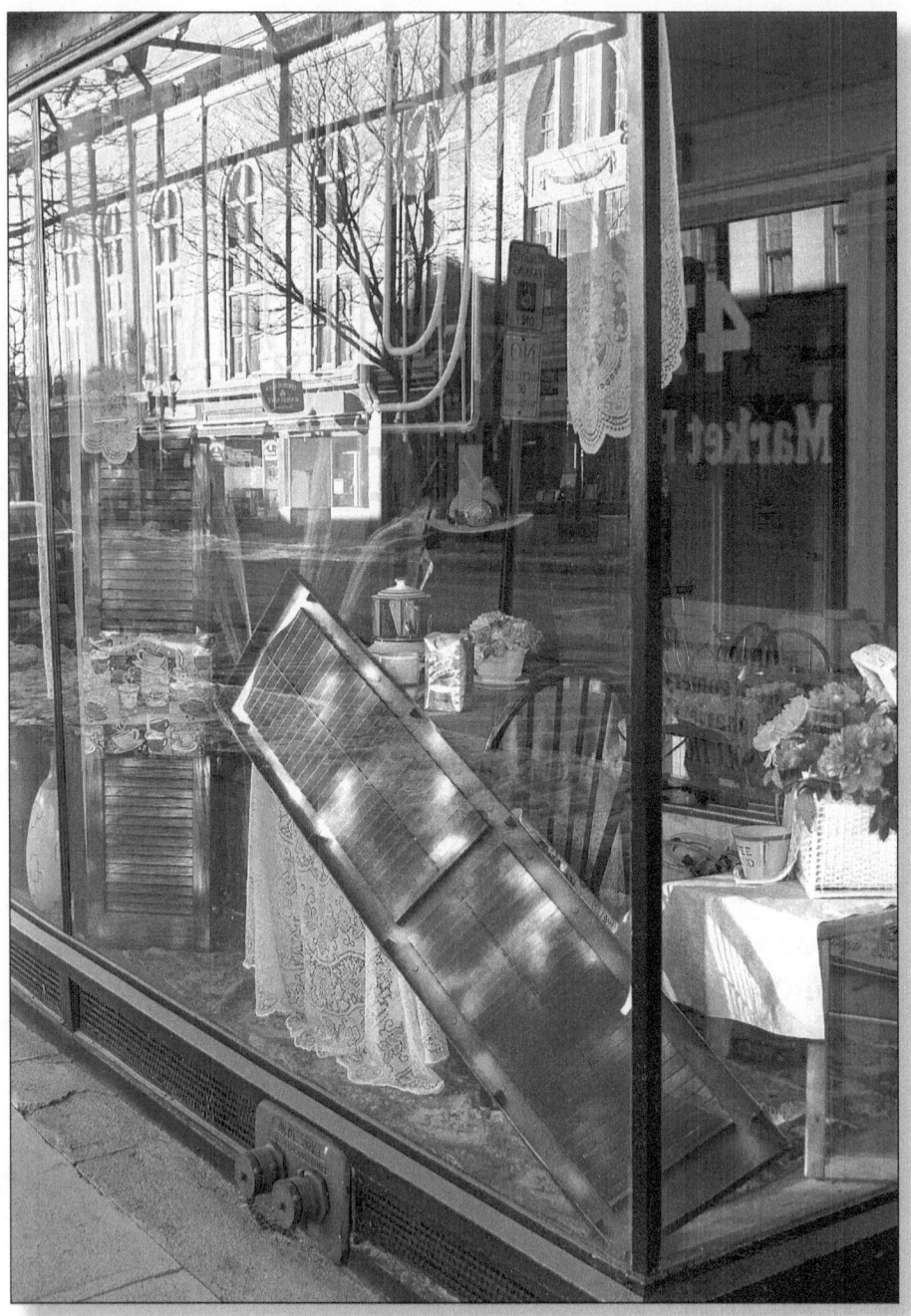

Gloversville, N.Y., March 16, 2014.
Canon EOS 10D, 28mm, f/5.6, 1/60, ISO 200, Tv, center-weighted metering.
Photo © 2014 by Shawn M. Tomlinson

All of the DSLRs mentioned can use older film lenses. You will not get as wide an angle with these lenses on these cameras as you would on a film SLR, but we're staying within budget.

So, the choice really is, for your first lens, whether you want a zoom lens or a prime lens.

Most people just starting out with DSLRs want the flexibility of a zoom lens, but if sharpness in your images is of primary concern, a fixed-focal length prime lens is a better choice.

You can always move closer or farther away yourself with a prime, rather than being lazy and letting the zoom lens change the apparent distance.

Prime lenses for the cameras listed with approximate used-market prices include:

1) Pentax: smc Pentax 50mm f/1.8 DA. Price: $139
2) Nikon: Nikkor AF D 50mm f/1.8. Price: $84
3) Canon: Canon EF 50mm f/1.8. Price: $79
4) Sony: Minolta Maxxum 50mm f/1.7. Price: $45

Better-than-kit zoom lenses for the cameras listed include:

1) Pentax: smc Pentax 28-70mm f/4 FA AL. Price: $69
2) Nikon: Nikkor G 28-100mm f/3.5-5.6. Price: $53
3) Canon: Canon 28-80mm f/3.5-5.6 II USM. Price: $45
4) Sony: Minolta Maxxum 28-105mm f/3.5-4.5. Price: $56

It is possible to save more money on zooms with greater range by buying third-party lenses.

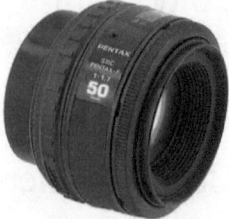

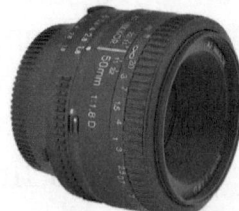

Prime or fixed-focal length lenses once were the standard for all SLRs. During the autofocus revolution — which coincided with a big push for the consumer market — the zoom lens became the standard for most people. Primes generally are sharper and have better glass for the money.

smc Pentax 50mm f/1.8 DA

Nikkor AF D 50mm f/1.8

These primes, when used on film SLRs give the same view through the camera as you would see without looking through it. With crop-sensor DSLRs recommended here, and the 1.5 crop factor, these lenses give the equivelant of 75mm. This typically is known as a "portrait" focal length because it is used for portraits. The reason? It gives sharp focus on the subject and nicely blurs the background. To get the same effect of a "normal" lens on a crop-sensor DSLR, you would need to use 35mm lenses, which gives you 52.5mm.

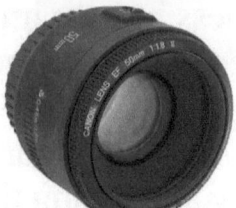

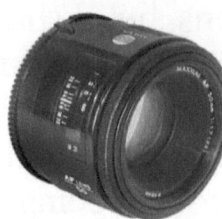

Apart from sharpness, the other great thing about prime lenses is they are much brighter than zooms and allow you to shoot much better images in low light.

Canon EF 50mm f/1.8

Minolta Maxxum 50mm f/1.7

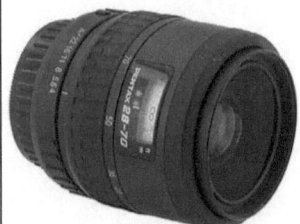

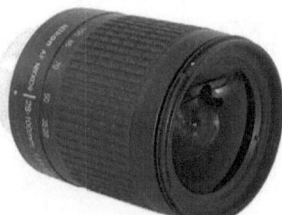

Zoom lenses, without a doubt, are far more versatile than prime lenses. They can give you "reach" meaning you can photograph you can't get closer to without you personally moving. At longer focal lengths, they produce a visual compression effect that can work very well and gives a different perspective than what the human eye sees. These zoom lenses give a slightly wide-angle-to-moderate telephoto range.

smc Pentax 28-70mm f/4 FA AL

Nikkor G 28-100mm f/3.5-5.6

Canon 28-80mm f/3.5-5.6 II USM

Minolta Maxxum 28-105mm f/3.5-4.5

The smc Pentax 28-70mm f/4 FA AL lens gives a true focal length of 42-105mm. It is recommended because of the constant maximum aperture, something most zooms in this price range do not have.

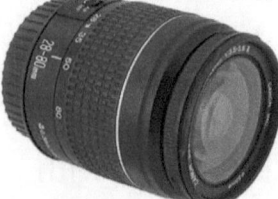

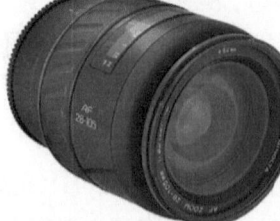

The Nikkor G 28-100mm f/3.5-5.6 gives a 42-150mm.

The Canon 28-80mm f/3.5-5.6 II USM gives a 44.8-128mm range because it has a 1.6x crop factor.

The Minolta Maxxum 28-105mm f/3.5-4.5 gives a 42-157.2mm range.

In general, third-party lenses are not quite as good as those made by the camera manufacturer, but if you stay away from the low end, most of them are fine.

There were many now-defunct third-party lens makers or at least distributors from JC Penney to Kmart. The most common low-end lenses are labeled Quantaray or Promaster. It is safer simply to remember the third-party names of the companies that produce good lenses. These are: Sigma, Tamron and Tokina.

These third-party lenses will work and give you great images. In most cases, however, especially for zoom lenses, buying used camera maker lenses is quite cheap.

The lenses listed have good glass and good sharpness, better than the kit lenses.

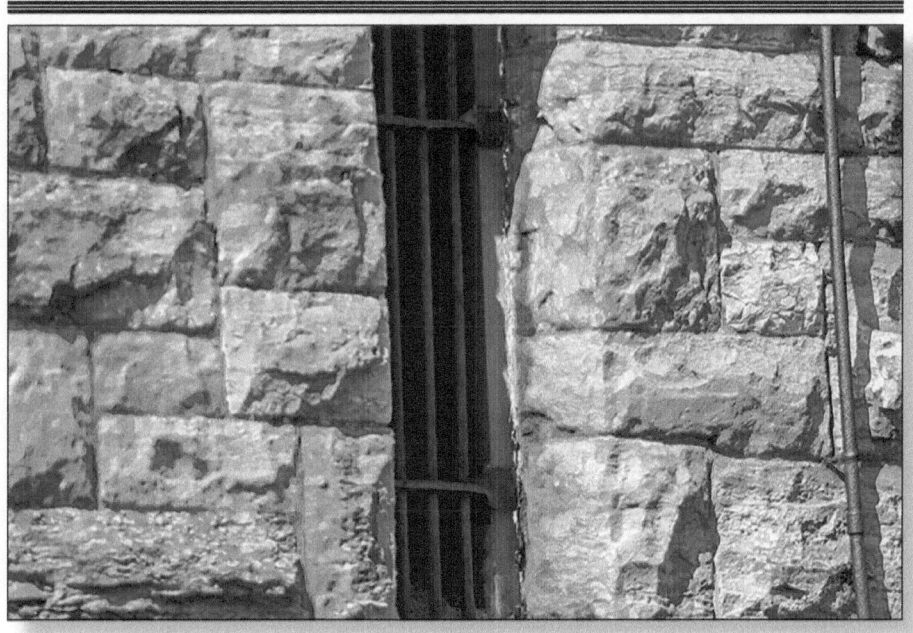

Amsterdam, N.Y., March 11, 2014.
Nikon D70, 300mm, f/4.5, 1/1250, ISO 200, Tv, pattern metering.
Photo © 2014 by Shawn M. Tomlinson

The trade off is that none of them have the wide-angle range when used on crop-sensor DSLRs.

We're just getting started though.

These lenses are the best, least expensive way to get shooting with a DSLR.

You can buy better lenses with more range later, especially once you determine what you like to shoot most.

For example, I shoot with a 28-80mm lens on both the Nikon D70 and the Canon EOS 10D.

These two lenses, similar to those mentioned on the shopping list, are sharper, better lenses than the 18-55mm kit lenses I could have gotten.

Well, for the Nikon. The Canon EOS 10D does not accept "digital" lenses, indicated by the EF-S designation on Canon lenses. The Canon EOS 10D only uses EF lenses.

When I'm shooting, 90 percent of what I photograph is covered by these lenses.

The other 10 percent of the time, I wish I had a wider angle or more reach with a telephoto.

My solution usually is to also carry my Pentax K20D with the Sigma 18-200mm lens to use for that 10 percent.

That lens also is better, sharper than an 18-55mm, but not as good as shorter focal length or prime lenses made by Pentax.

Crop Factor

Most consumer DSLRs have a CCD or CMOS sensor that produces images smaller than the 35mm film standard. The effect is that the sensor records only the center section of what the lens sees and essentially makes the image appear more telephoto than wide. For Nikon, Pentax and Sony the crop factor is 1.5. (Canon is a bit smaller.) This means that any focal length lens must be multiplied by 1.5 in order to determine what the focal length would be on the 35mm film frame standard. So, an 18mm lens, multiplied by 1.5, would be 27mm. This still is wide angle, but not as wide as it sounds. In 35mm terms, a 50mm lens is "standard" because the images it sees are the same size as what you see with your eye. On a crop-sensor or APS-C DSLR, this is 75mm or a portrait telephoto. To get a standard view on this type of camera, you need a 35mm (52.5mm) lens.

The advantage of this is that you get more "reach" with a telephoto. An 18-200mm lens gives you 27-300mm on a crop-sensor DSLR.

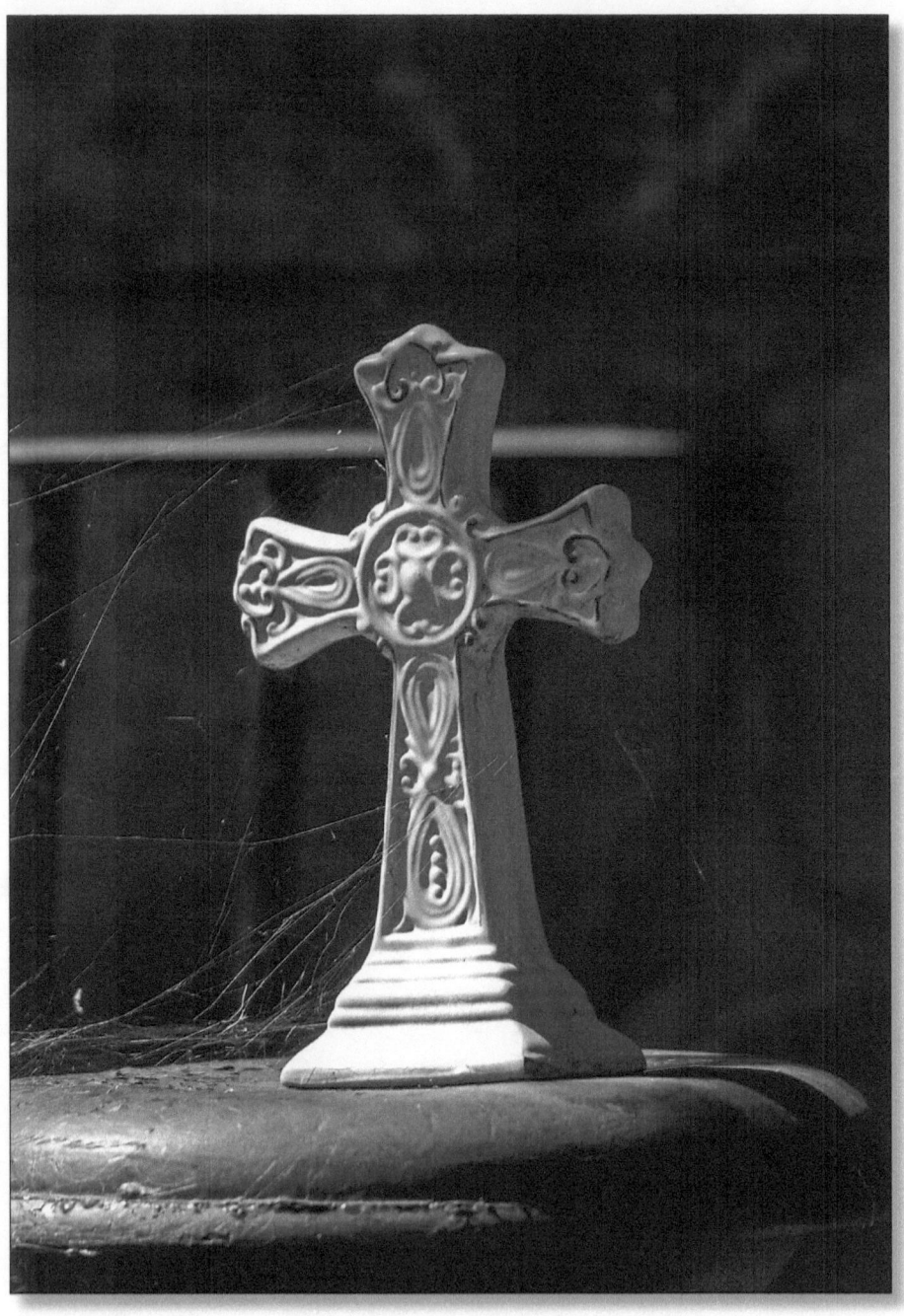

Ballston Lake, N.Y., Sept. 4, 2013.
Pentax *ist DS, 200mm, f/5.6, 1/500, ISO 200, P, center-weighted metering.
© 2013, 2015 Shawn M. Tomlinson

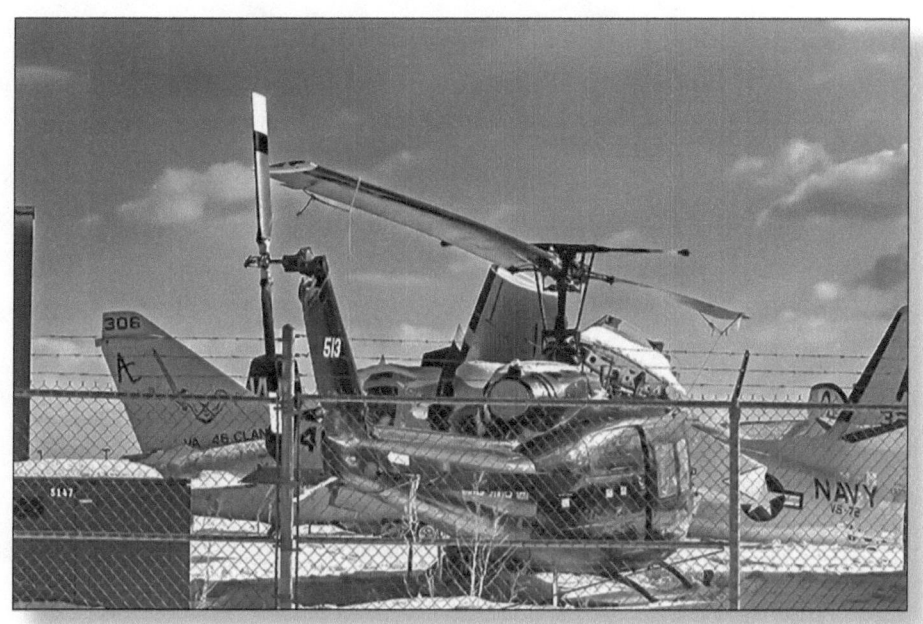

Glenville, N.Y., Feb. 10, 2014.
Nikon D70 66mm, f/11, 1/500, ISO 200, P, pattern metering.
© 2014, 2015 by Shawn M. Tomlinson

Part 6:

What Else Do I Need?

If you buy a DSLR on eBay or another such site, you may or may not get the extra stuff you need to start shooting.

Trust me on this.

I bought an ancient Nikon D1 that did not come with a charger but did come with a dead battery.

I only discovered this after I won the auction. I paid, including shipping, $58 for a camera that once cost $6,000. What a steal! Except... the charger, when you can find one costs around $100. A battery costs anywhere from $100 for a Nikon one down to $20 for a third-party unit. To make the camera work, I needed to spend another $120, bringing the total to $178. Had I just bought the thing from KEH, I would have received a working battery and the charger with the camera for $109. A "good deal" isn't always what it seems.

1) Make certain you get the charger and a working battery with the camera you purchase, or make certain that buying these items separately will not exceed the total of what you could have gotten the package for from a reputable dealer.

2) Check to find out what type of memory card the camera uses. These rarely come with old DSLRs and they are not all the same. Most modern DSLRs at the

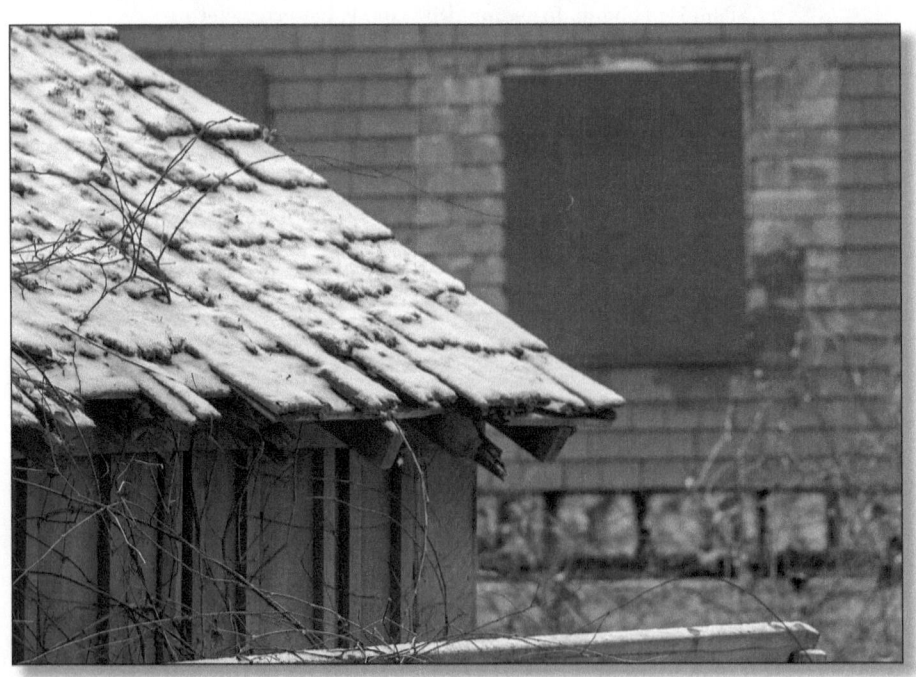

Saratoga Springs, N.Y., Dec. 10, 2013.
Pentax *ist DS, 200mm, f/8, 1/500, ISO 200, P, center-weighted metering.
© 2013, 2014 Shawn M. Tomlinson

sub-pro level use SecureDigital or SD cards. Older DSLRs often use CompactFlash or CF cards. Here's what the recommended cameras use:

A) Pentax *ist DS: SD card. Note that you may need to upgrade the firmware — free from Pentax — to use SD cards with capacities greater than 1gb.

B) Nikon D70: CF card. Note that Nikons do not always work with off-brand memory cards. Nikon recommends Lexar and SanDisk for the D70. I also have a Transcend that works fine, but a Maxell causes problems.

C) Canon 10D: CF card.

D) Sony A100: CF card.

I have not found any capacity limitations with the Pentax (with the free firmware upgrade), Nikon or

Checklist Rehash

1) Working charger
2) Working battery
3) Memory card
4) Camera strap
5) UV or haze filter
6) Gadget bag
7) Cleaning kit

Canon models, and have yet to try the Sony. I know that the Nikon D1 I bought, being from the last century, can only handle up to 2gb and Nikon does not offer a firmware upgrade.

3) Take a look at the manual for your DSLR before it arrives to determine the type of strap it requires*. Not everyone uses camera straps, but they do offer a way to secure the camera to your body while shooting. If your camera does not come with a strap, you may want to buy one separately.

4) Confirm the filter size of the lens you bought and get a UV or haze filter for it immediately. Don't wait. Lens caps are for amateurs, but every pro or semi-pro or aspiring pro needs a protection filter on the front of the lens. If the filter gets broken, it is a lot cheaper to replace. Note that, like the quality of the lens, the quality of the filter glass also is vitally important. Top glass brands that also aren't that expensive include Hoya, Tiffen and Canon. If you buy the lens from KEH, Adorama or B&H, it will have the filter size listed alongside the lens.

Fitting the Budget

These prices are current as of this writing, but often change on the used market. They are meant as a rough guide of what you will pay.

Pentax *ist DS:
1) Camera body (6.1mp): $100
2) Battery and charger (included at KEH)
3) 16gb SanDisk SD card: $10
4) Pentax camera strap: $10
5) 52mm Tiffen UV filter: $11

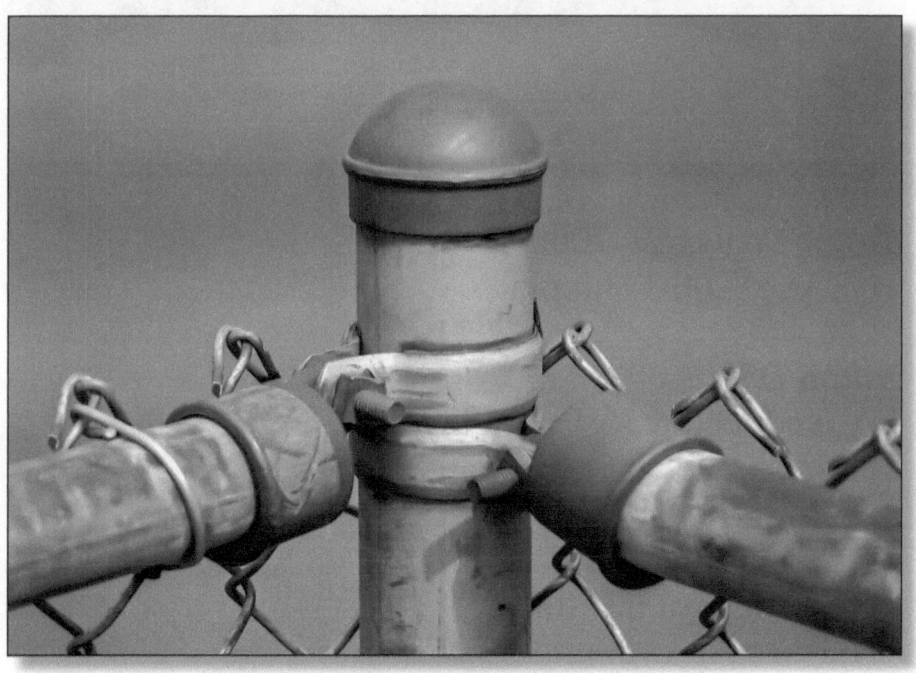

Rexford, N.Y., April 1, 2014.
Canon EOS 10D, 63mm, f/5.6, 1/1000, ISO 200, M, center-weighted metering.
© 2015 by Shawn M. Tomlinson

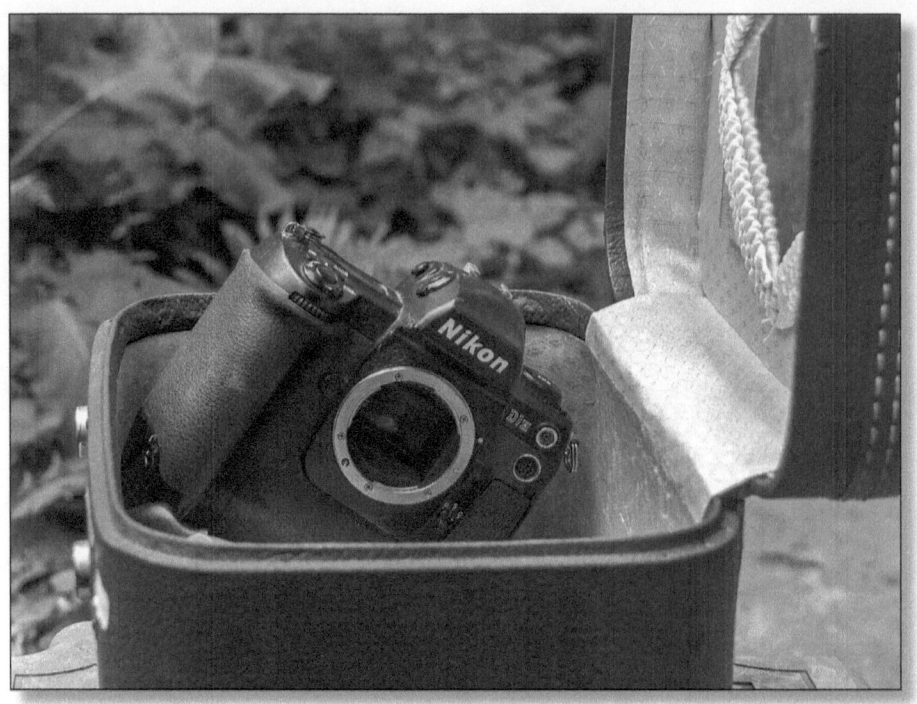

Saratoga Springs, N.Y., June 14, 2014.
Nikon D70, 70mm, f/7.1, 1/200, ISO 250, P, pattern metering.
© 2015 by Shawn M. Tomlinson

6) smc Pentax 28-70mm f/4 FA AL: $69
TOTAL: $200 + shipping

Nikon D70
1) Camera body (6.1mp): $89
2) Battery and charger (included at KEH)
3) 8gb CF Lexar card: $11
4) Nikon camera strap: $11
5) 58mm Hoya UV filter: $9
6) Nikkor AF D 50mm f/1.8: $84
TOTAL: $204 + shipping

Canon EOS 10D
1) Camera body (6.1mp): $62
2) Battery and charger (included at KEH)
3) 8gb CF Lexar card: $11
4) Canon camera strap: $11
5) 58mm Hoya UV filter: $9
6) Canon 28-80mm f/3.5-5.6 USM: $45
TOTAL: $138 + shipping

Sony A100
1) Camera body (10.2mp): $119
2) Battery and charger (included at KEH)

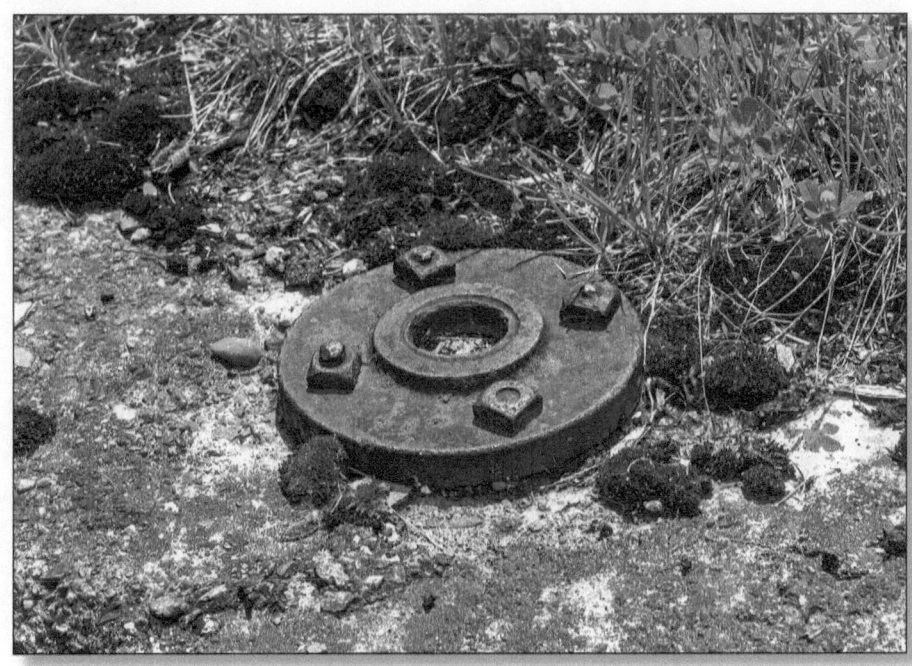

Greenwich, N.Y., June 14, 2014.
Nikon D70, 80mm, f/11, 1/500, ISO 250, P, pattern metering.
© 2015 by Shawn M. Tomlinson

3) 8gb CF Lexar card: $11
4) Sony camera strap: $6
5) 62mm Tiffen UV filter: $12
6) Minolta Maxxum 28-105mm f/3.5-4.5: $56
TOTAL: $204 + shipping

In each case, the total, even with shipping, comes in below our budget limit, so we can consider some additional accessories.

Gadget bag
Not good to leave that DSLR out on the end table gathering dust. A gadget bag will keep it safe along

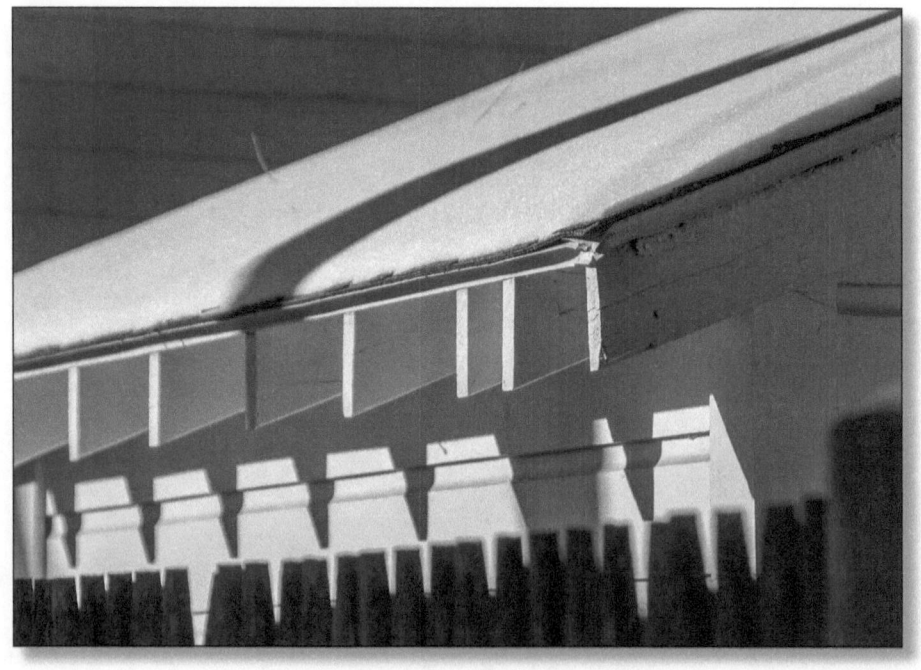

Saratoga Springs, N.Y., Jan. 10, 2015.
Sony A100, 150mm, f/6.3, 1/400, ISO 200, Tv, pattern metering.
© 2015 by Shawn M. Tomlinson

with the lens, battery, charger and memory card.

Again, brand names are essential here because a DSLR does not fit in your shirt pocket and needs a safe place to be when you're not using it.

I prefer Tamrac, but even small ones are expensive. Tenba and Lowepro also are popular and are well made.

• Cost: $25-$100

Extra battery

Unlike the old days when you could just pop into a drug store or depart-

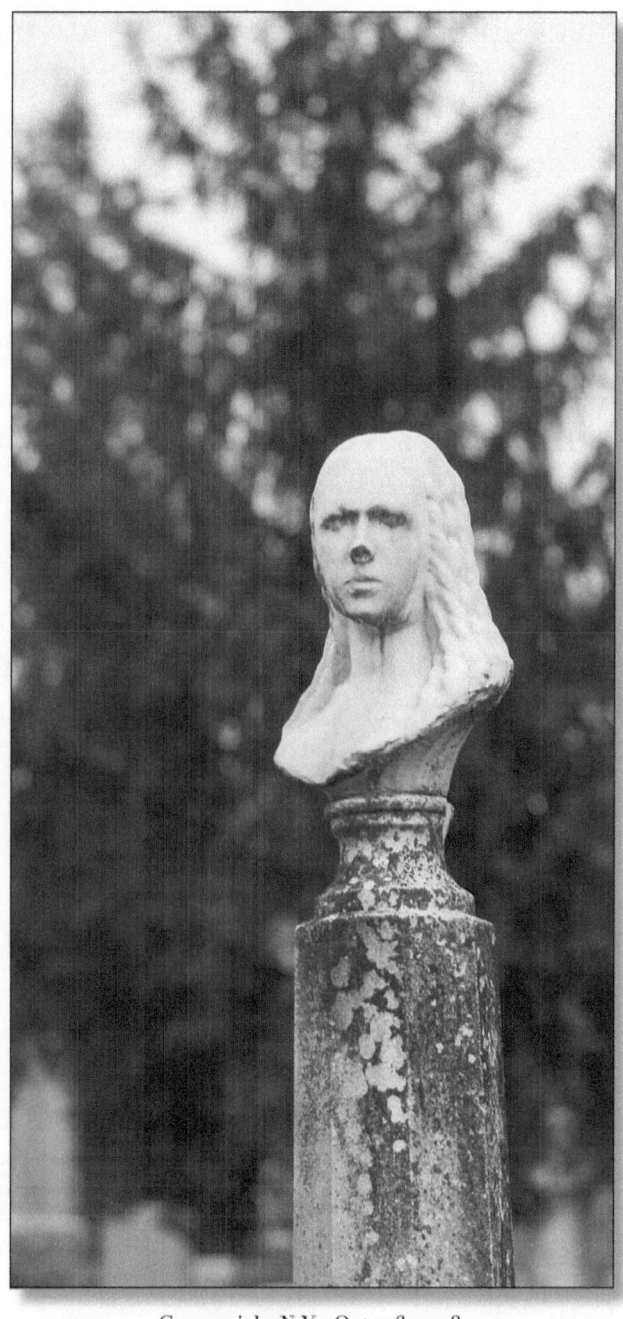

Greenwich, N.Y., Oct. 26, 2013.
Pentax *ist DS, 153mm, f/6.7, 1/250, ISO 400, P, center-weighted metering.
© 2013, 2015 by Shawn M. Tomlinson

ment store and pick up a battery if yours ran out, today there are so many batteries local stores — unless you are fortunate enough to live near an actual camera store — don't carry them. It's always a good idea to have a second battery.
• Cost: $12-$20

Extra memory cards
These days, they don't cost much and it's a good idea to keep several in your gadget bag as a backup.
• Cost: $5-$20

Polarizer
In this era of Photoshop, photographers don't often use filters as they once did, but a polarizer can come in handy. It deepens the blues in the sky and often makes other colors — such as leaves — pop. Get one the same size as your UV filter.
• Cost: $20-$40

Sensor cleaning kit
The sensor is going to get dirty.
Especially when you add another lens to your package and start changing between them.
There are very high-priced sensor cleaning kits, but I've found that I can do the job cheaper.
The first kit I bought at the Dollar Tree cost $1. The second kit, with the correct swabs for the APS-C sensor, cost $20.
• Cost: $1-$20

Battery grip

I used to think that having a battery grip on my DSLR made me look pretentious.

And it probably does.

However, the battery grip at least doubles your battery life by containing or using two batteries.

These are not available for the Pentax *ist DS (if you see one on eBay, it is for the film SLR Pentax *ist), nor for the Nikon D70 (you need a D70S for a grip; current used cost for the Nikon D70S: $99; for a thrid-party grip: $96).

You can get a very inexpensive grip for the Canon EOS 10D and a third-party one for the Sony A100.

• Cost: $20-$100

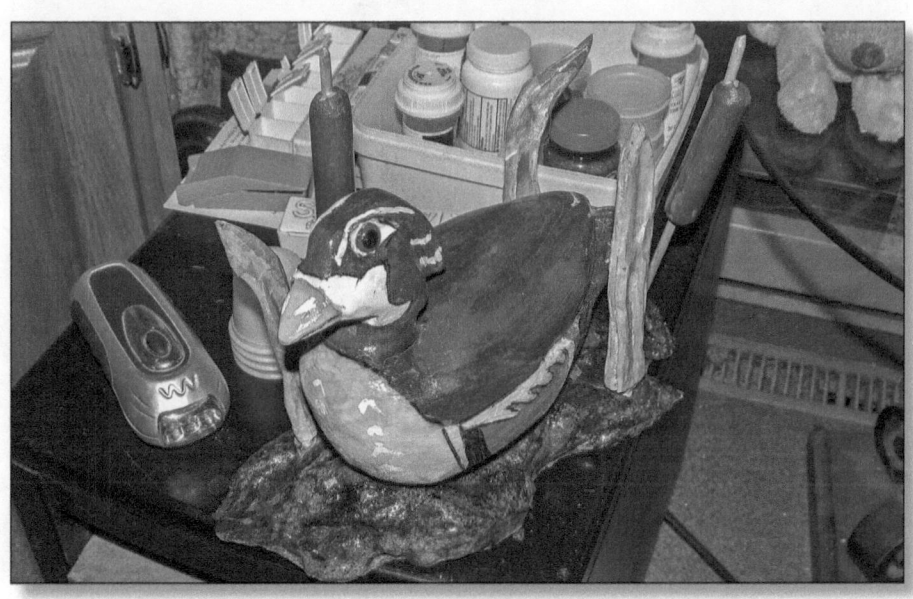

Broadalbin, N.Y., April 4, 2014.
Canon EOS 10D, 28mm, f/11, 1/200, ISO 200, M, pattern metering.
© 2014, 2015 by Shawn M. Tomlinson

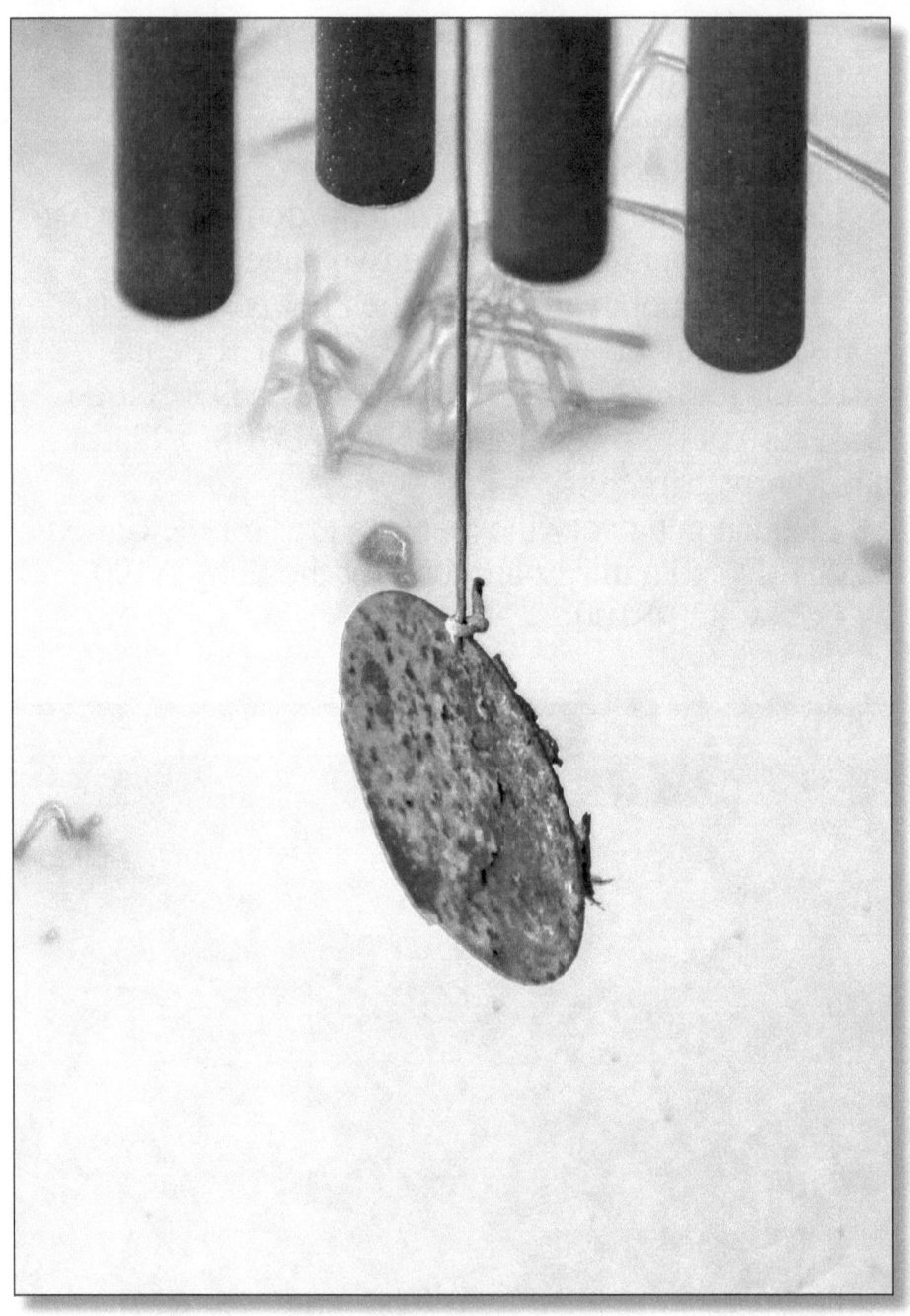

Ballston Lake, N.Y., Jan. 9, 2015.
Sony A100, 300mm, f/6.3, 1/320, ISO 125, Tv, pattern metering.
© 2015 by Shawn M. Tomlinson

NOISE!

Noise is annoying.

That's, I suppose, why we call it noise instead of a symphony.

In film photography, we always were battling film grain.

The higher the ASA/ISO speed of the film, the more grain appeared. Now, some retro photographers appreciate the classic grain look of films such as Kodak Tri-X Pan. You can even add film grain in Photoshop.

In digital photography, because it is digital, you get noise rather than grain. In some DSLRs, this noise resembles grain and that's not so bad.

The lower the light, however, the more likely the noise will produce red-green-blue (RGB) artifacts which look terrible.

In very low light, this RGB noise exists in a form called banding; straight bands of color noise across a part or all of the frame.

There's not much you can do about banding if it occurs. Shake your head and move on to the next image.

For regular RGB artifact noise, there are several things you can do to fix it.

First, avoid it. You can do this by ALWAYS shooting in RAW and ALWAYS shooting in the lowest possible ISO sensitivity for your scene. RGB artifacts do not typically appear until you reach 800 ISO and higher unless you're shooting in the dark. Shooting at 100, 200 or 400 in most cases will prevent the appearance of these artifacts.

Second, if you use Photoshop — and a serious photographer does not use Photoshop Elements because it's designed to take care of you — or Lightroom, you can filter most or all of the RGB artifacts.

In Photoshop CC's Camera RAW interface, choose the Details button (it looks like two steep pyramids) and use the Color slider under Noise Reduction.

In Lightroom, select the Develop tab and scroll down to Detail, then use the Color slider under Noise Reduction.

I've managed to rescue many old photographs I shot — when I was stupid enough to use high ISO sensitivities and shot in JPEG — with these tools.

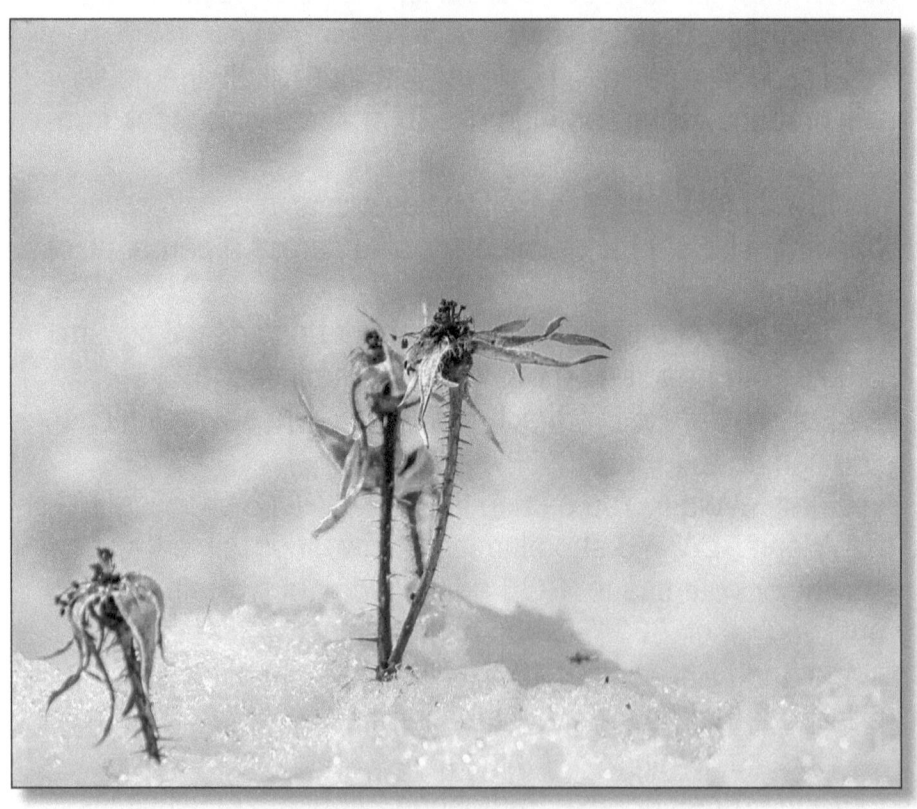

Ballston Lake, N.Y., Feb. 24, 2015.
Sony A100, 300mm, f/9, 1/400, ISO 200, Tv, pattern metering.
© 2015 by Shawn M. Tomlinson

Part 8

It Came in the Mail. Now What?

You just got back inside after a mad dash to the mailbox for your "new" old DSLR. Congratulations!

Now what?

Here are some guidelines for DSLRs in general, followed by some specific to the cameras mentioned previously.

General Procedures

1) Before the DSLR arrives, search online for the manual for your particular model.

Most of them are available from the manufacturers' websites.

These are old cameras, so the camera makers may not keep the manuals available forever.

Read the manual on your computer, if you like, but it is best to print it to have easy access while you get to know your DSLR.

2) Unpack the camera, the accessories and the lens.

Look them over and make sure they are not damaged. If they are, the main used camera dealers — KEH, Adorama and B&H — all have return policies to replace damaged equipment or refund your money.

3) Place the battery in the charger and plug it in. You can't do anything until the battery is charged, so go peruse other DSLRs and lenses online while you wait.

4) Install the battery.

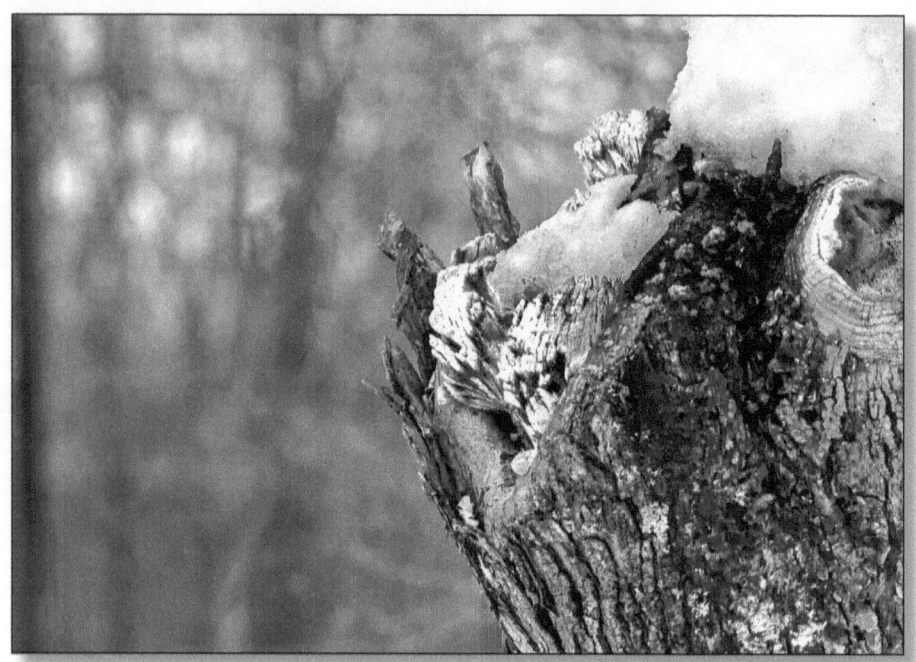

Ballston Lake, N.Y., March 4, 2015.
Pentax *ist DS, 200mm, f/5.6, 1/350, ISO 400, Tv, spot metering.
© 2015 by Shawn M. Tomlinson

5) Install the memory card.

6) Format the memory card.

7) Attach the UV filter to the lens. Carefully.

8) Attach the lens to the camera body. Carefully.

9) Set the camera's image quality to RAW.*

10) Set the camera's ISO to the lowest available: 100 or 200.**

11) Take test shots of your cat or dog.

12) Get out and shoot.

* Amateurs shoot in JPEG. JPEG is a compressed file format that by its nature leaves noise and artifacts in images. Shooting everything in RAW — ALWAYS

— significantly decreases noise and artifacts, plus it gives you lots of options when you edit your photos later. RAW takes up more memory card and hard drive space, but it produces much better images.

** ALWAYS use the lowest ISO sensitivity setting possible for the lighting situation. 100 or 200 ISO is perfect for sunlight. Well, 200 really is the best for good light because it has a better dynamic range — better and wider color rendition — than lower ISOs in DSLRs. Some DSLRs even go down to 50 ISO, but not those recommended here. The 100 ISO setting is fun to experiment with, but you'll likely find that 200 ISO is the best for you.

You may need to raise it inside without a flash. Remember that the higher the ISO number, the greater the noise and artifact level.

The best way to get the best images from any DSLR, but particularly these older models, is to:

1) ALWAYS shoot in RAW.

2) ALWAYS shoot at the lowest possible ISO number.

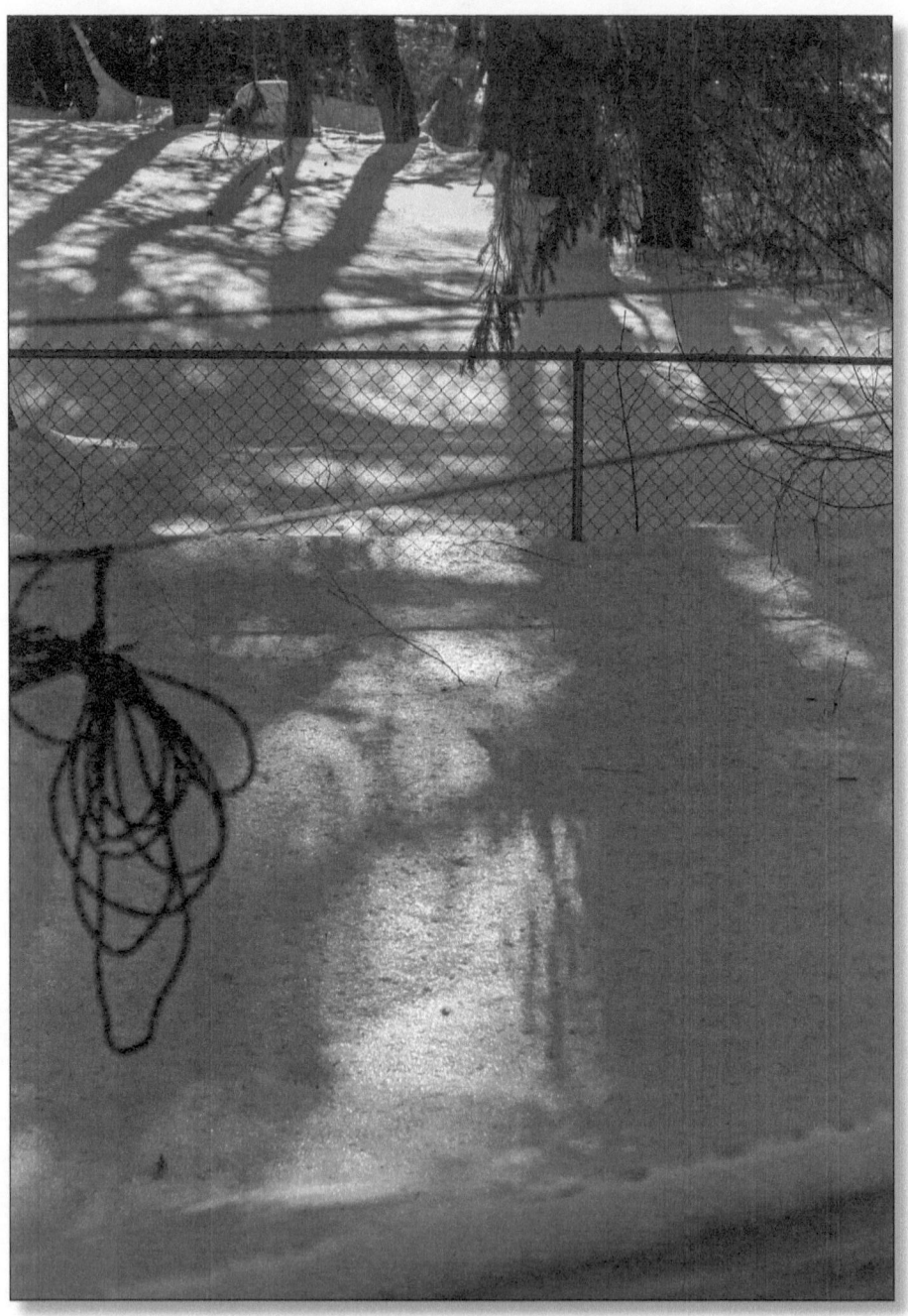

Ballston Lake, N.Y., March 6, 2015.
Sony A100, 50mm, f/4.5, 1/4000, ISO 400, Tv, pattern metering.
© 2015 by Shawn M. Tomlinson

Dust

The worst bane for digital single-reflex cameras is dust.

We never had this problem with film. Well, lenses got dirty, but they were relatively easy to clean.

The one advantage fixed-lens point-and-shoot digital cameras have over DSLRs is that you can't get dust on the sensor from changing lenses because you can't change lenses.

The flexibility of DSLRs that allows a wide range of lenses also allows dust to settle on the sensor. This appears as gray or black spots on your images, particularly in sky photos.

The one problem I had when I bought the Nikon D70 was that the sensor got dirty and my daily cleaning of it — which I shouldn't have to do — kept making it worse.

Everyone will warn you that it is dangerous to clean the sensor yourself. It's a good warning. You could potentially damage or destroy it if you are not very careful.

But you're not really cleaning the sensor anyway. There is a plastic or glass filter in front of the sensor that decreases moire (the strange effect you can get when photographing things with line patterns) and this is what has the dust. You can clean it.

But... BE VERY, VERY CAREFUL.

Until I got a sensor cleaning kit, I tried everything. Swabs, lint-free cloths, and many other things it's best not to mention.

Actually, the one thing that mostly worked was a smartphone cleaning kit I got at the Dollar Tree for $1.

Then the kit came. It has the best cleaning liquid to use on special swabs. Although these are expensive, I recom-

---

mend getting such a kit if you are going to clean the sensor yourself.

And it hardly seems worth it to spend $200+ on professional cleaning services for a camera that costs $100 or less.

Modern DSLRs have dust reduction systems, but honestly, they don't work that well. I still need to clean the sensors.

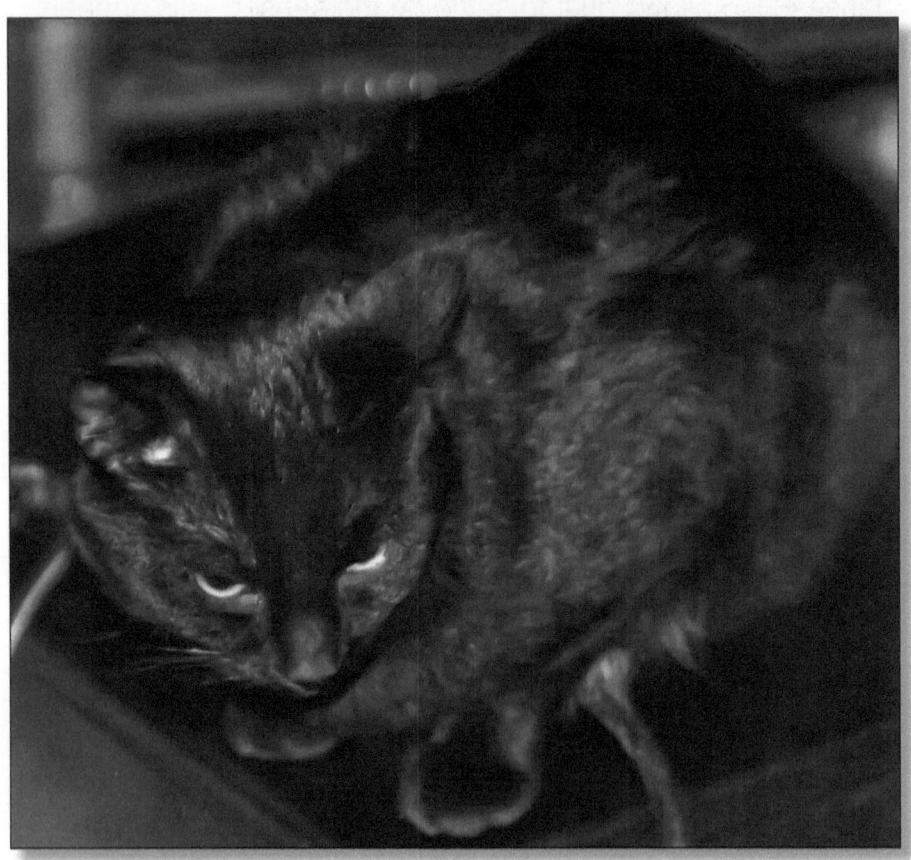

H.P. Lovecraft, Ballston Lake, N.Y., Jan. 9, 2015.
Sony A100, 70mm, f/4, 1/50, ISO 400, Tv, pattern metering.
© 2015 by Shawn M. Tomlinson

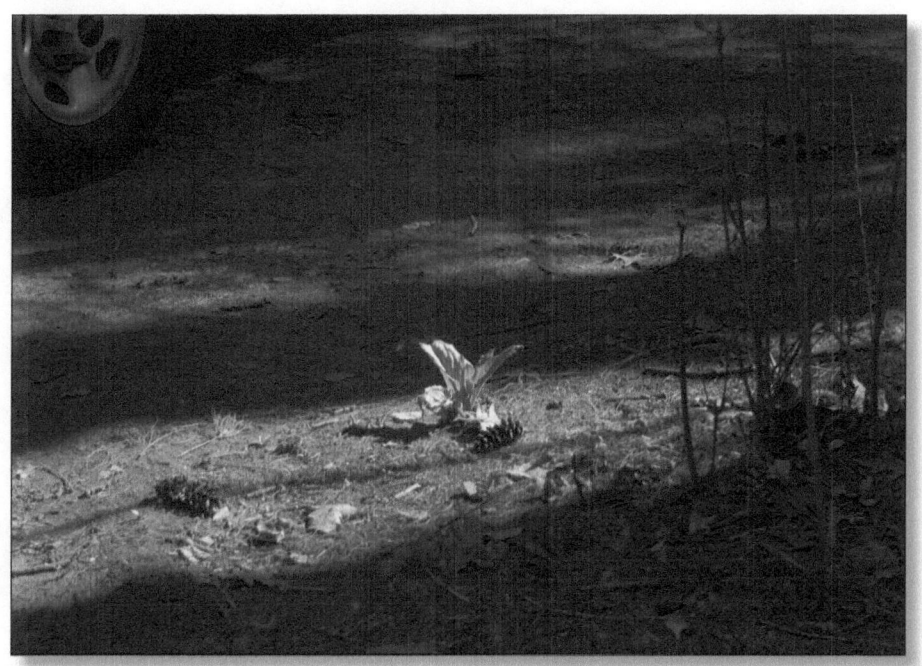

Yaddo, Saratoga Springs, N.Y., May 1, 2013.
Pentax *ist DS, 55mm, f/6.7, 1/125, ISO 200, P, spot metering.
© 2013, 2015 by Shawn M. Tomlinson

Part 9:

The Future's So Bright... I Gotta Use a Polarizer

You already had a passion for serious photography before we started this trip.

Now you have some of the basic tools to fulfill that passion.

Some may stop with one of these camera packages and not buy another DSLR until this one falls apart. Or ever.

Others will see what fantastic images they can pro-

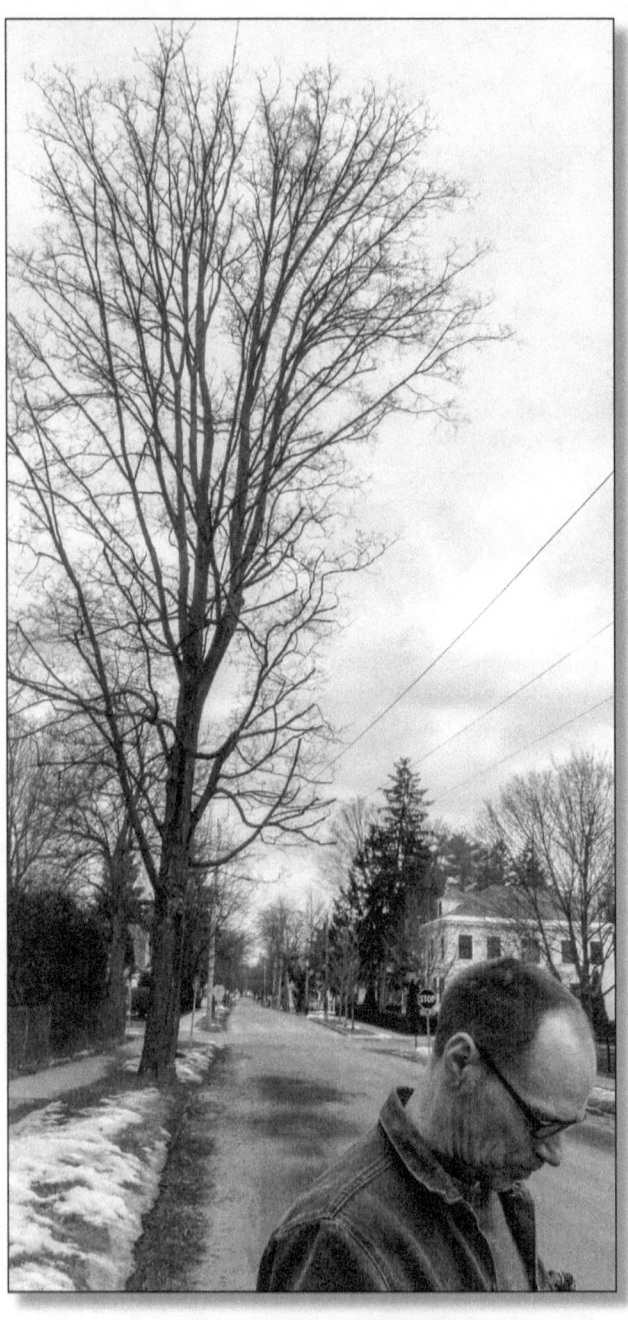

Gary W. Ziroli, Saratoga Springs, N.Y., March 11, 2013.
Pentax *ist DS, 18mm, f/22, 1/125, ISO 6400, Tv,
pattern metering.
© 2013, 2015 by Shawn M. Tomlinson

duce and want to try other inexpensive DSLRs. That's what I did. Up until this experiment, I planned to always stay with Pentax. Afterward, I debated Nikon and Canon and gave up on Pentax as my main camera. That has become the Nikon D7000, which I can't say enough good things about, but it exceeds the budge here. For the price of one modern DSLR and a lens, you basically can get all four of the camera packages recommended here and use them all to produce great photos.

Using these older DSLRs may allow you to discover which camera best suits you and which produces the images you like best. It always is possible to fix color and other aspects of digital images in Photoshop, but it is a joy to open Adobe Bridge and see that the majority of your photos already look great.

This is what happened with the Canon EOS 10D for me. I like the blues and reds better than the Pentax or Nikon, and better than the Sony A100 samples I've seen. You may not agree. You may like the subtler

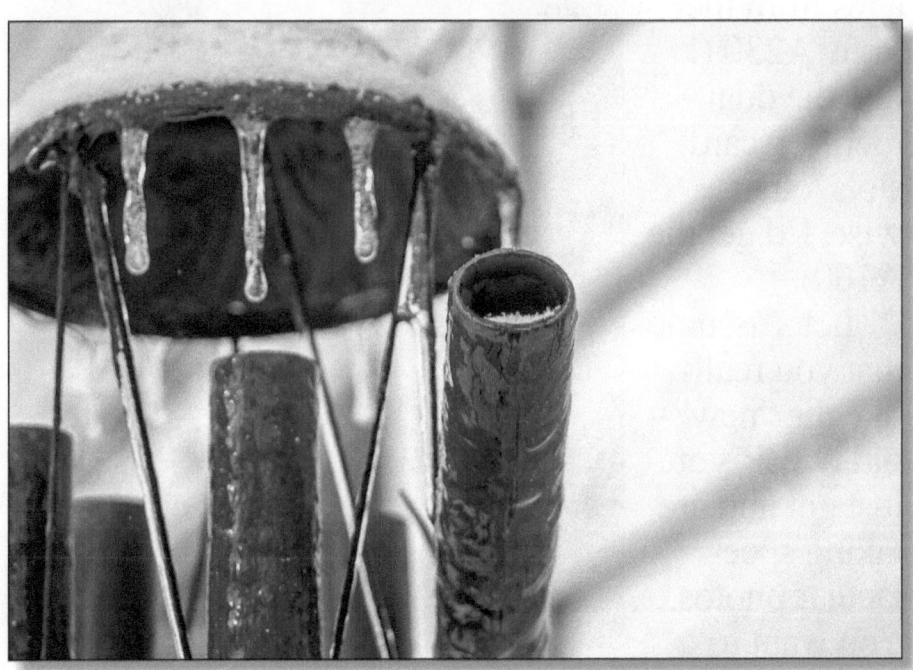

Ballston Lake, N.Y., March 13, 2014.
Canon EOS 10D, 80mm, f/5.6, 1/350, ISO 200, M, pattern metering.
© 2014, 2015 by Shawn M. Tomlinson

blues of the Pentax or the green-ish-yel-low-ish-ness of the Nikon.

Honestly, I get great images from the Pentax *ist DS, the Nikon D70 and the Canon EOS 10D, and believe I will get great images from the Sony A230 (I like the dual memory card slots, otherwise, I'd get the A100).

Let's assume that you really like the "new" old DSLR you just got and are taking spectacular photos. You want to expand a bit, though, so

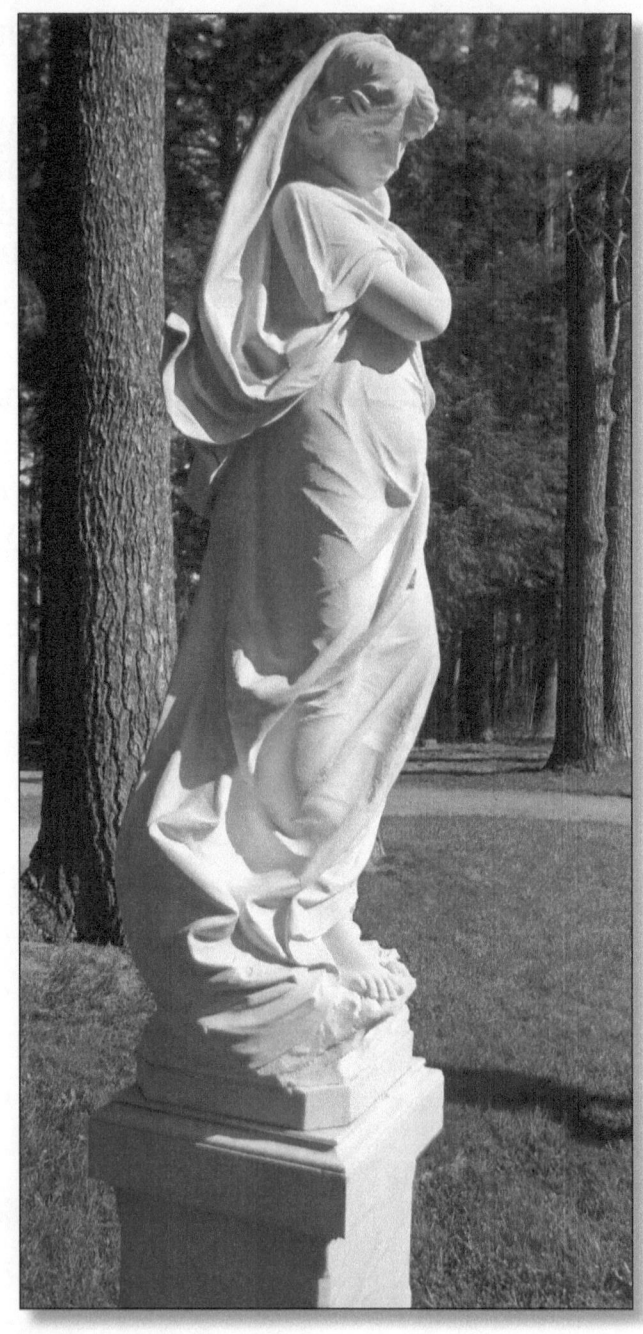

Yaddo, Saratoga Springs, N.Y., May 1, 2013.
Pentax *ist DS, 18mm, f/5.6, 1/3000, ISO 200, P, spot metering.
© 2013, 2015 by Shawn M. Tomlinson

what's next?

The main thing emphasized by me and most other photographers is to get better lenses.

One consideration, though, before you start buying, is: Is this the camera brand I'm likely to stay with? If the answer is yes, then you can start looking at some really serious glass. The reason is that really good lenses will improve the images from the DSLR you already have, and you will be able to use them on the next and better DSLR you buy.

In other words, if you buy, for example, the Nikon D70 and start spending a lot on good lenses, you will

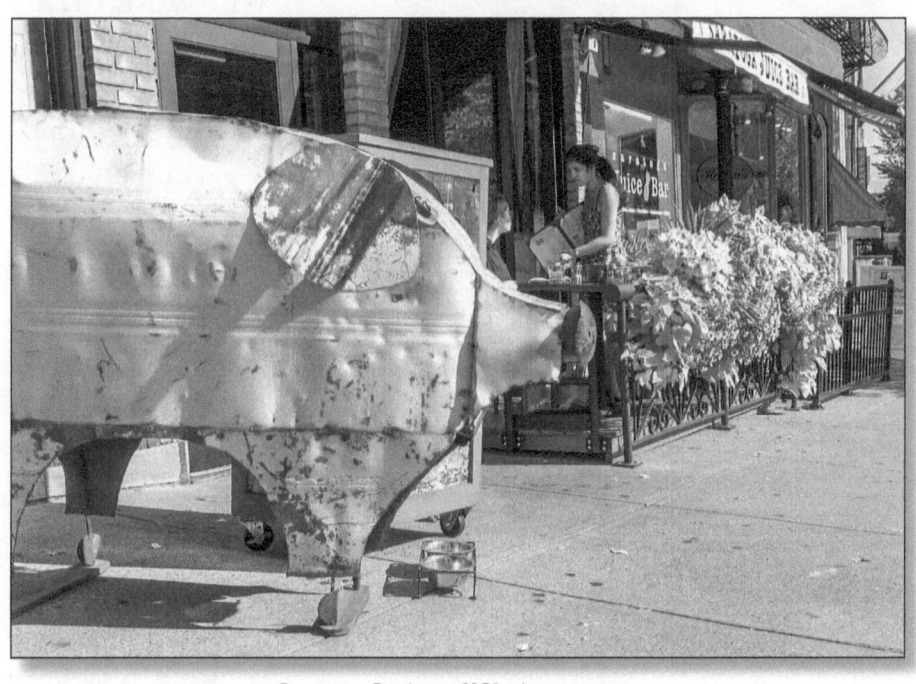

Saratoga Springs, N.Y., Aug. 2, 2014.
Nikon D70, 18mm, f/5.6, 1/320, ISO 200, P, pattern metering.
© 2014, 2015 by Shawn M. Tomlinson

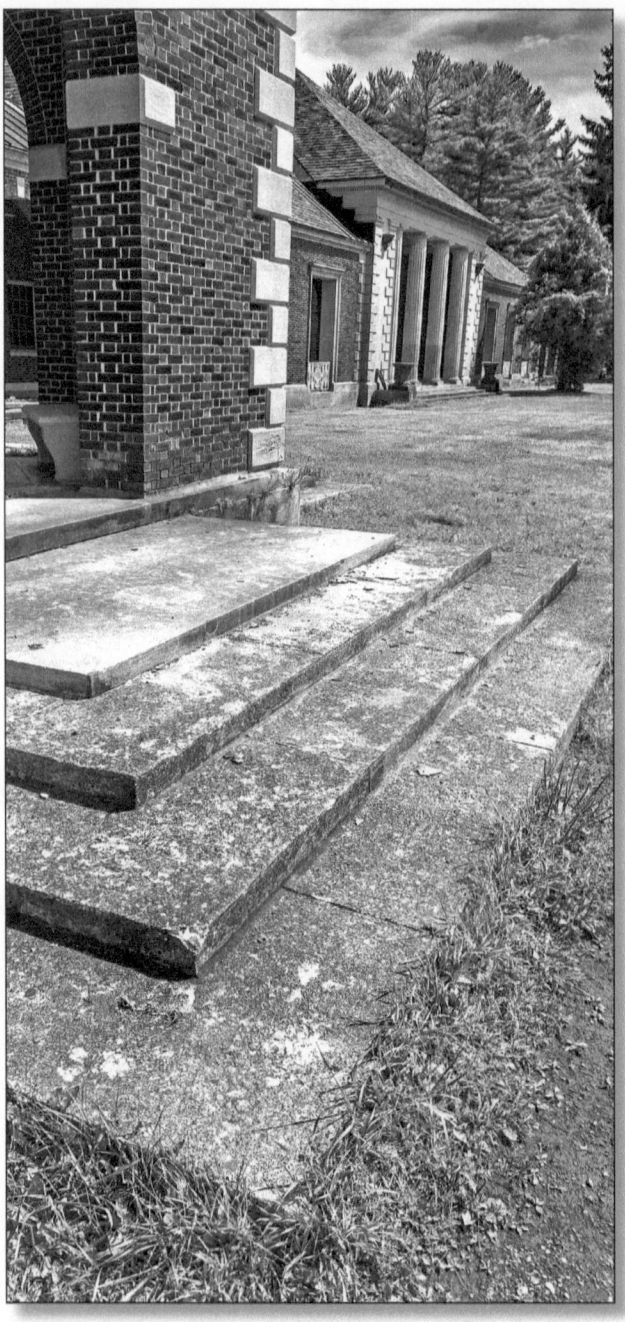

Roosevelt Baths, Saratoga Springs, N.Y., Aug. 2, 2014.
Nikon D70, 18mm, f/10, 1/400, ISO 200, P, pattern metering.
© 2014, 2015 by Shawn M. Tomlinson

have to start all over again if you switch to Pentax, Canon or Sony. This is what is happening to me now as I make the major photography-life choice to move to Nikon. None of my Pentax lenses will work on a Nikon DSLR body. This is another good reason to try all four DSLRs recommended: You get to choose a camera before you start putting serious money into a system.

Camera manufacturers make a wide variety of lenses at a wide variety of glass quality. Although better lenses tend to cost more, price is not always indicative of the best quality. Some very expensive lenses are less sharp and have more aberrations than cheaper ones.

So what should you buy?

It depends on which lens you bought to start. If you bought a prime lens, the next one probably should be a zoom, and vice versa. To get a standard, wide coverage with lenses, there are several ways you can go. You can get an all-in-one super zoom that covers 18-200mm (27-300mm) for each of these cameras except the Canon EOS 10D. Such a lens, though convenient, does compromise quality of images somewhat. My Sigma 18-200mm is not nearly as sharp as my smc Pentax F 80-200mm.

Here's a basic guide for buying the focal length of lenses you may find useful:

1) 16mm prime: This gives you 24mm on a crop-sensor DSLR.

2) 24mm prime: This gives you 36mm on a crop-sensor camera, so it is a moderate wide-angle.

3) 35mm prime: You can use this type lens to give your crop-sensor DSLR a normal view of 52.5mm on the Pentax, Nikon and Sony, or 56mm on the Canon.

4) 50mm prime: This is a portrait lens on these cameras of 75mm.

5) 18-70mm or 18-135mm zoom: These usually are better lenses than the kit 18-55mm lenses and give a good but moderate zoom range.

6) 55-200mm zoom: This gives you the old film SLR standard of approximately 82.5mm to a super

zoom of 300mm.

7) 100-300mm zoom: 200-450mm in SLR terms.

For a basic, crop-sensor DSLR, a good package for the least money would be:

1) 35mm prime

2) 18-105mm zoom

3) 100-300mm zoom

These will cover the full range from moderate wide-angle to super telephoto.

How and what you shoot should determine what lenses you buy. For example, if you shoot a lot of landscapes, you probably want the widest angle lenses you can get. If you mainly photograph individual or small groups of people, normal to portrait lenses are best. For wildlife or other distance photography, you need the longest zoom you can get.

You'll learn what you need as your style develops.

In the meantime, with your basic DSLR package, get out there and shoot.

And shoot and shoot and shoot.

— SMT

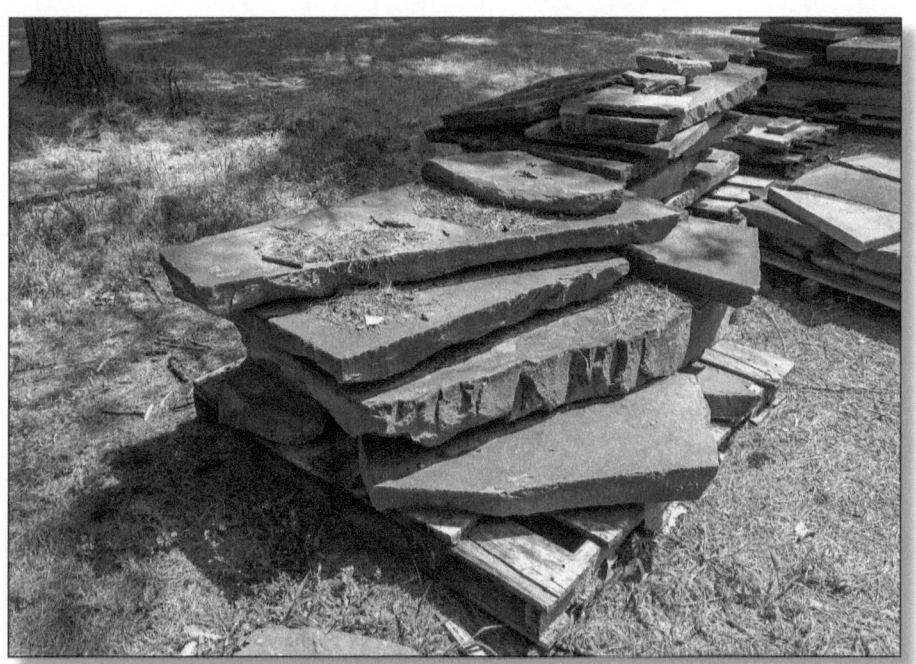

Roosevelt Baths, Saratoga Springs, N.Y., Aug. 2, 2014.
Nikon D70, 18mm, f/10, 1/400, ISO 200, P, pattern metering.
© 2014, 2015 by Shawn M. Tomlinson

Part 10:
Notes & Stuff

Not all the answers are here, obviously.

And you may wonder (or not) what my credentials are to tell you all this stuff and why you may want to take any of it seriously.

So, OK.

I started with my Dad's Kodak Instamatic when he wasn't looking. It was, at the time, an expensive camera and he didn't want a little kid breaking it. Then, somewhere along the line, I became obsessed with the idea of instant photography, probably because we had many film cartridges lying around that we never had developed.

So, I talked my parents into buying me a $100+ Polaroid 420 Land Camera in the early 1970s. It was great, but as a pre-teen, I really didn't have the money to keep buying the film. The camera went largely unused.

By the mid-1970s, I had discovered the photography magazines — Modern Photography, Popular Photography, Petersen's Photographic... there were a lot of them then — and started to drool over 35mm SLRs. Of course I wanted the Nikon or the Minolta, or the

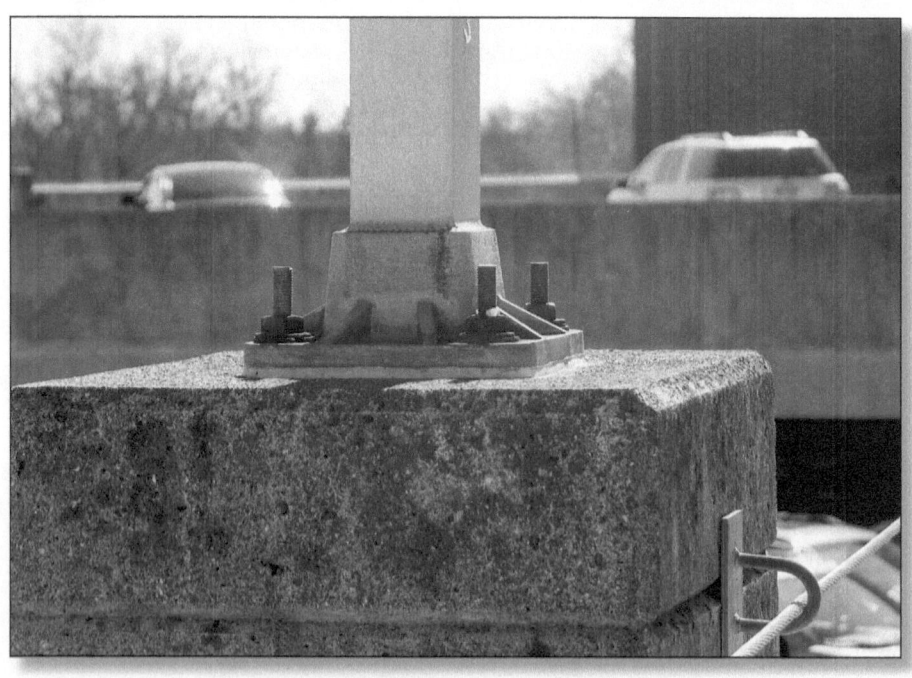

Ellis Hospital, Schenectady, N.Y., March 18, 2014.
Canon EOS 10D, 80mm, f/8, 1/250, ISO 200, P, pattern metering.
© 2014, 2015 by Shawn M. Tomlinson

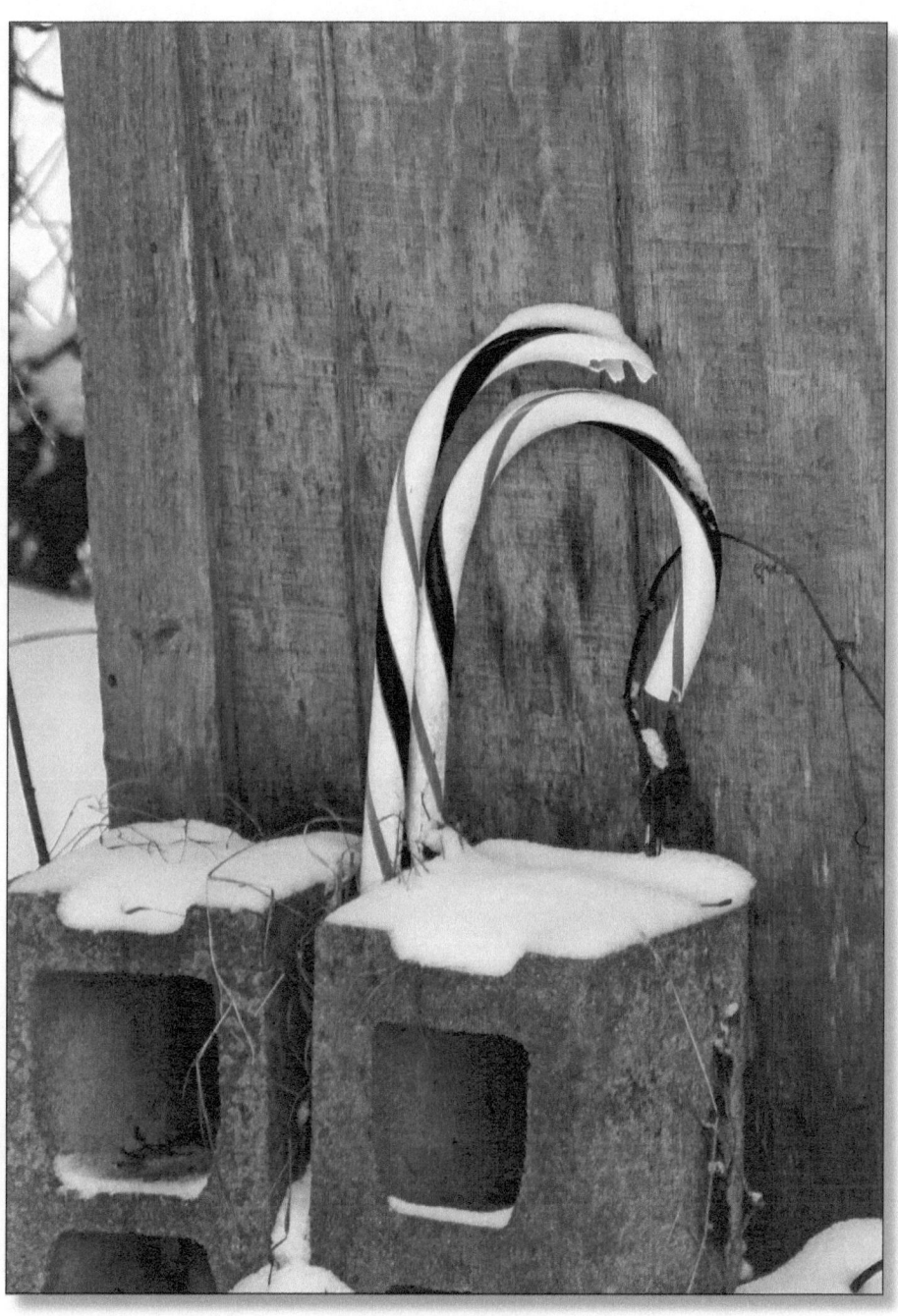

Ballston Lake, N.Y., Jan. 9, 2015.
Sony A100, 300mm, f/6.3, 1/500, ISO 320, Tv, pattern metering.
© 2015 by Shawn M. Tomlinson

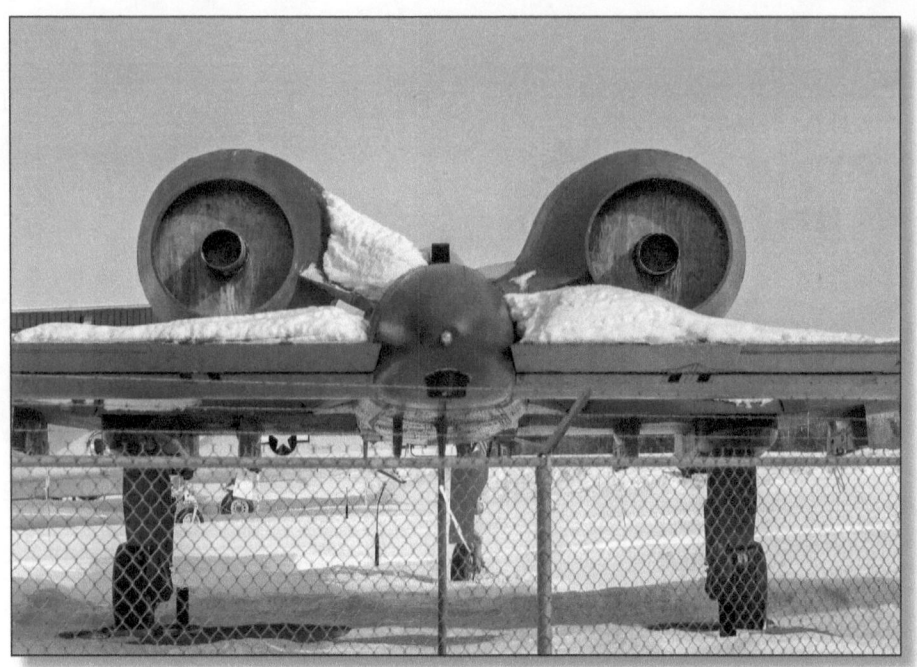

Air Museum, Glenville, N.Y., Feb. 26, 2015.
Sony A100, 50mm, f/5.6, 1/3200, ISO 200, Tv, pattern metering.
© 2015 by Shawn M. Tomlinson

then-new and terribly revolutionary Olympus OM-1. I also found, though, a review of a cheap Soviet knock-off SLR called a Cosmorex SE. That made a lot more sense. It cost less than $100, which my parents could ill-afford, but they did.

I loved my Cosmorex SE and shot everywhere with it. I assembled my own darkroom with an enlarger and accessories for $15 from a garage sale in the cellar and got to work. I never was good at making prints with an enlarger, but I could develop film reasonably well.

A few years later, I developed a fascination for the Pentax MX fully manual yet through-the-lens metered SLR that was the first of the Pentax smaller cameras.

All the camera makers were producing smaller SLRs in the trend started by Olympus.

When I got that Pentax MX, I was in heaven. The lens was much better, the metering was through that lens so I could set exposures without taking the camera from my eye. The Cosmorex had a meter cell stuck to the front of the pentaprism and I had to turn a dial to match the meter needle while looking straight down at the camera. Today, though, the Cosmorex does still have one advantage over most other cameras. It does not require a battery, so it will work all the time, even in really cold weather.

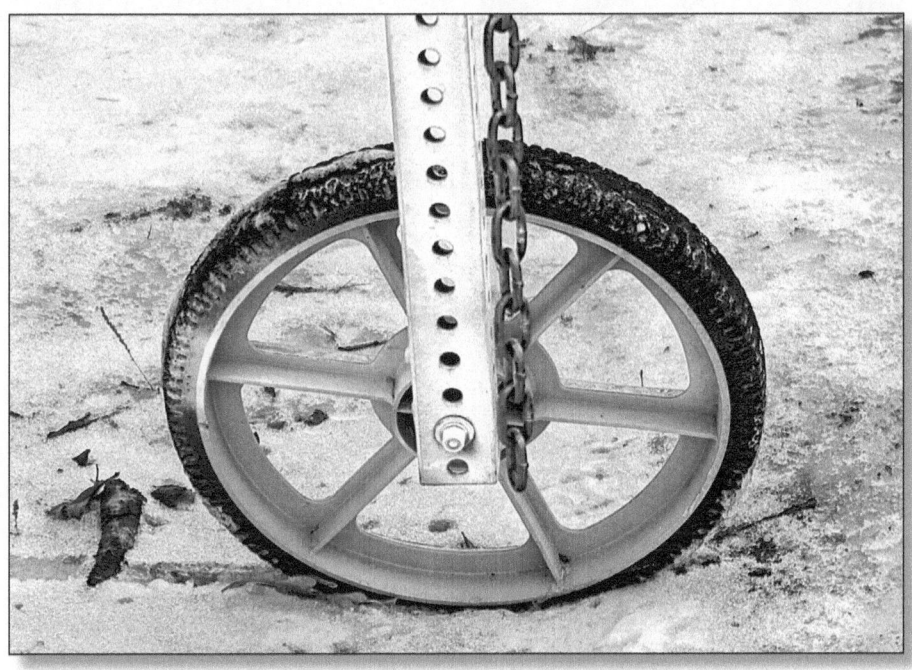

Indian Meadows Park, Glenville, N.Y., March 14, 2014.
Canon EOS 10D, 80mm, f/5.6, 1/90, ISO 100, P, pattern metering.
© 2014, 2015 by Shawn M. Tomlinson

Anyway, I liked the Pentax MX so much that years later when it came time to move to autofocus, I purchased the Pentax PZ-10 without doing much research. It was a great camera, too, but plasticy compared to the MX.

Naturally, when it was time for my first DSLR, I stuck with Pentax and bought that *ist DS.

I should backtrack here a bit and mention that not all this photography was just for my own use. In 1982 while at my first job as a newspaper editor, I shot a photo in a park that the publisher liked and used as the cover photo for the company's flagship newspaper.

From then on, I shot many photos routinely for the newspapers for which I worked, even though I was not employed specifically as a photographer; usually as a reporter and/or editor. This led to me publishing thousands of photos over the years.

Of course, as the editor, I could choose my own photos to print, but other editors did as well. As a Sunday and features editor, I also found that I could get a much better package on the page if I shot the photos myself. It also got me out of the office.

It was at that particular office in Gloversville, NY, that I first used a DSLR. The newspaper owned a then-relatively-new Nikon D1. It was massive and impressive and I loved it. I couldn't pry it out of the official photographer's hands very often, though, so I often shot with the Nikon D80, also owned by the newspaper. This led me to buying the Pentax *ist DS because I needed a DSLR for work and other stuff, and I always liked Pentax, and Nikon was too expensive, and I still irrationally hated Canon.

Much more recently, I started writing a lot of articles about photography, cameras (and Macintosh computers) for websites (as a pro, not as a blogger; in other words, I get paid for them) and that's where I started really considering other DSLRs.

I had become an expert with Photoshop out of necessity (the photographer at the newspaper rarely was around to process photos

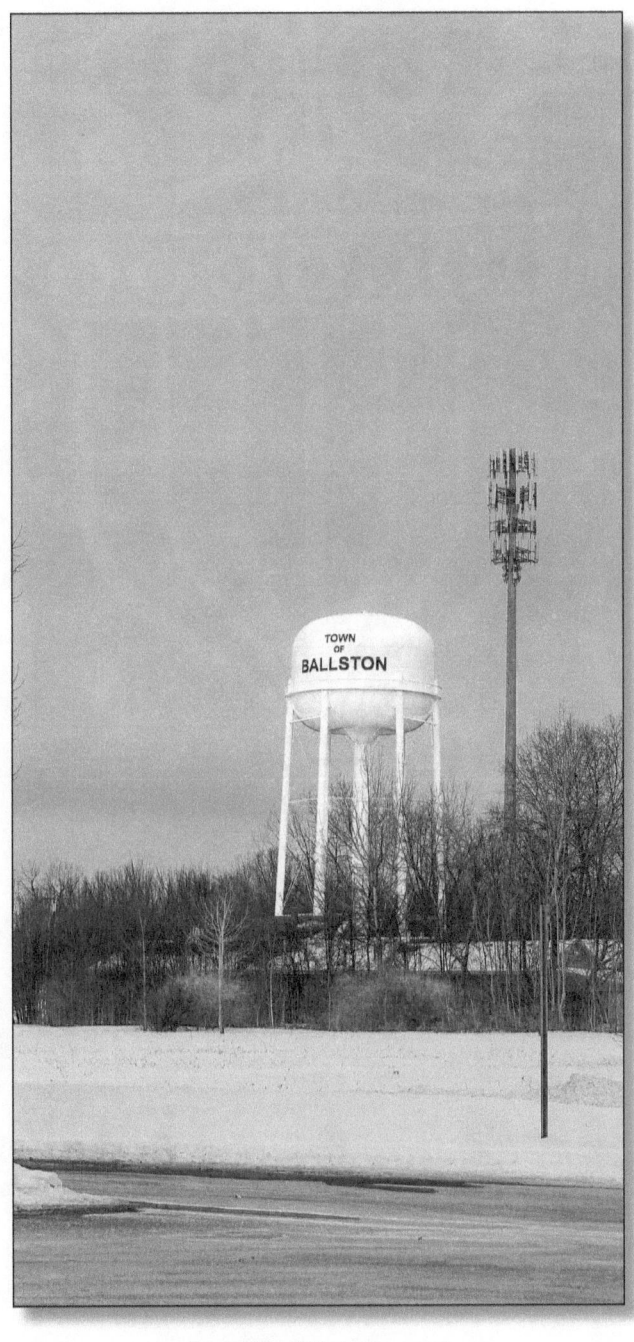

Burnt Hills, N.Y., Jan. 29, 2015.
Sony A100, 50mm, f/4.5, 1/640, ISO 200, Tv, pattern metering.
© 2015 by Shawn M. Tomlinson

Roosevelt Baths, Saratoga Springs, N.Y., Aug. 2, 2014.
Nikon D70, 250mm, f/5.3, 1/320, ISO 200, P, pattern metering.
© 2015 by Shawn M. Tomlinson

for me) and the knowledge I gained has been tremendously useful in my photography career.

And I still don't like Lightroom.

Then, I started acquiring old film SLRs I always had wanted at rock-bottom prices. I still like to shoot film (not develop it; I have drawers of film; but shoot it) and I could get serious SLRs for prices undreamed of previously. For example, when the revolutionary Nikon

F4S came out in 1988, the body by itself cost around $6,000. I got mine for $136 including shipping.

It was terribly fun to buy and use these old film cameras, but then, I realized I could get DSLRs cheaply as well.

Following my epiphany with the quality of the Pentax *ist DS last summer, I started looking around for other brands and found *all* of them very cheap.

This occurred because people buy into the megapixel Cold War I mentioned at the start and keep abandoning their old DSLRs in favor of the flashy new ones.

Hey, we're consumers, it's what we do.

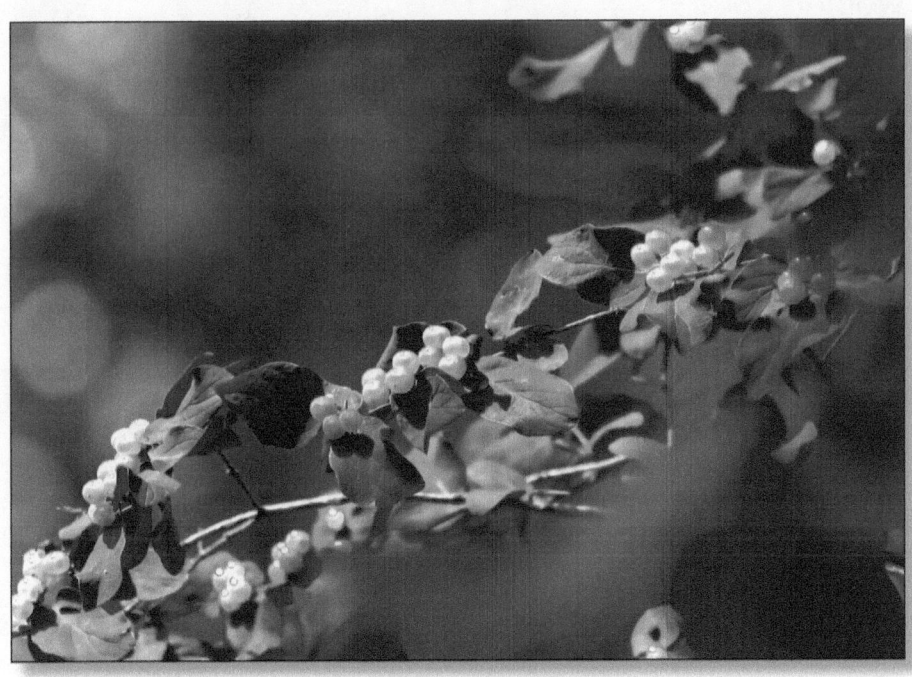

Mayfield, N.Y., Aug. 1, 2014.
Nikon D70, 300mm, f/6, 1/800, ISO 200, Tv, pattern metering.
© 2015 by Shawn M. Tomlinson

So no one wanted the old 6-megapixel cameras, but having just learned that the 6-megapixel Pentax *ist DS could produce amazing images, I was willing to take the chance.

Besides, I finally could shoot with a Nikon digital camera again, and I wanted to see if they were as great as I remembered they were.

From my experience, you can learn and move into serious photography with the aid of this book.

One more point, one I'm sure will come up, is about the brands and companies I've mentioned here.

I do not receive any money, equipment or consideration from Pentax, Nikon, Canon, Sony, Adobe, KEH, Adorama or B&H. I'm open to it, of course. Who wouldn't be?

But my point here is that I mention these companies purely from my experience and not to promote them.

If you are buying used, the camera makers get nothing from you anyway.

The other companies, the resellers, do.

I am mentioning them to help you, not them.

If you feel better buying on eBay or Amazon (also companies from which I get no kickback), go ahead.

My experience simply has shown me that, while I can get a good deal and a good product on either, I am safer and more assured when I buy from KEH, Adorama or B&H.

It's up to you to decide how you want to do it.

Good luck and see ya.

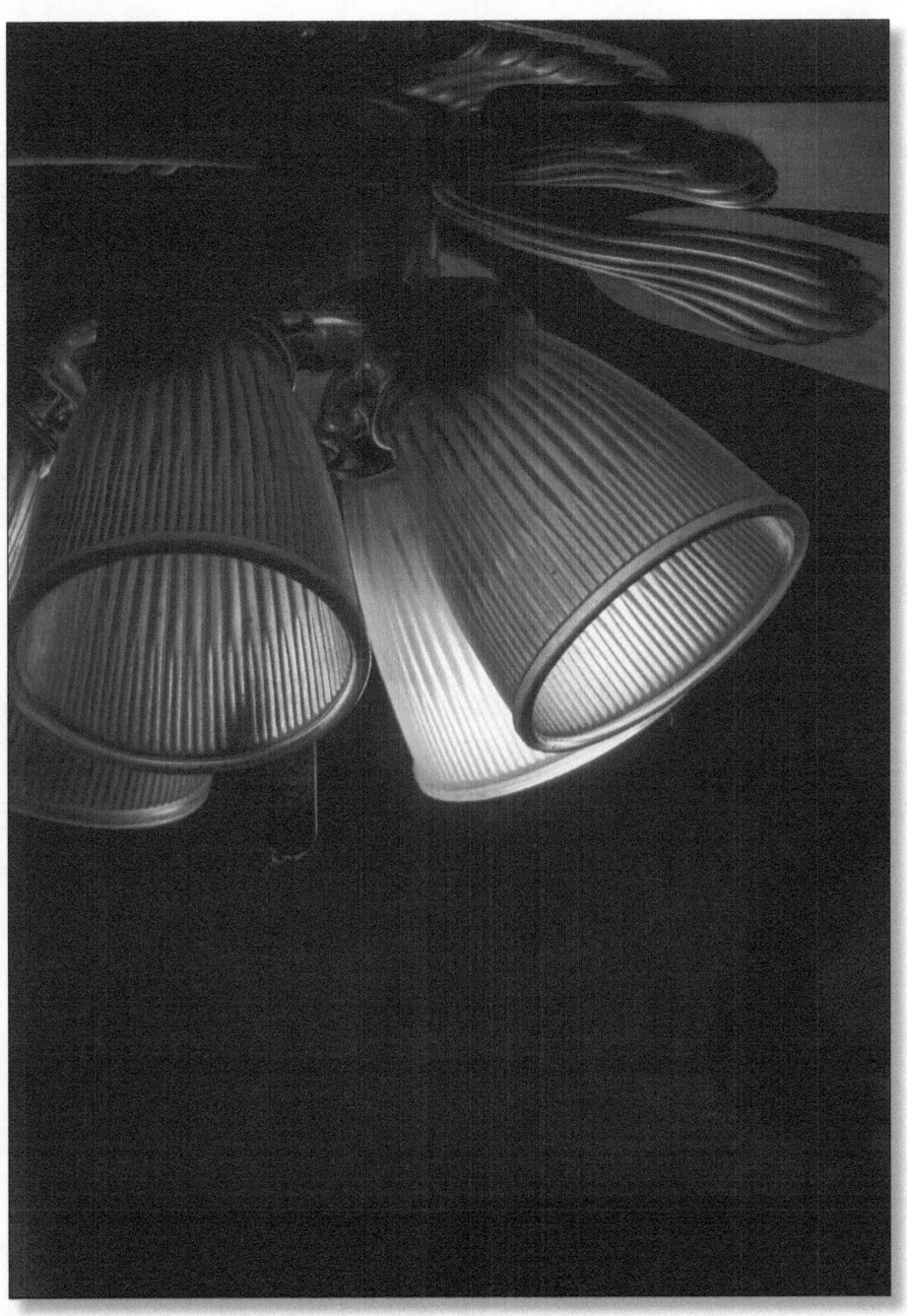

Ballston Lake, N.Y., Jan. 9, 2015.
Sony A100, 200mm, f/14, 1/30, ISO 200, Tv, pattern metering.
© 2015 by Shawn M. Tomlinson

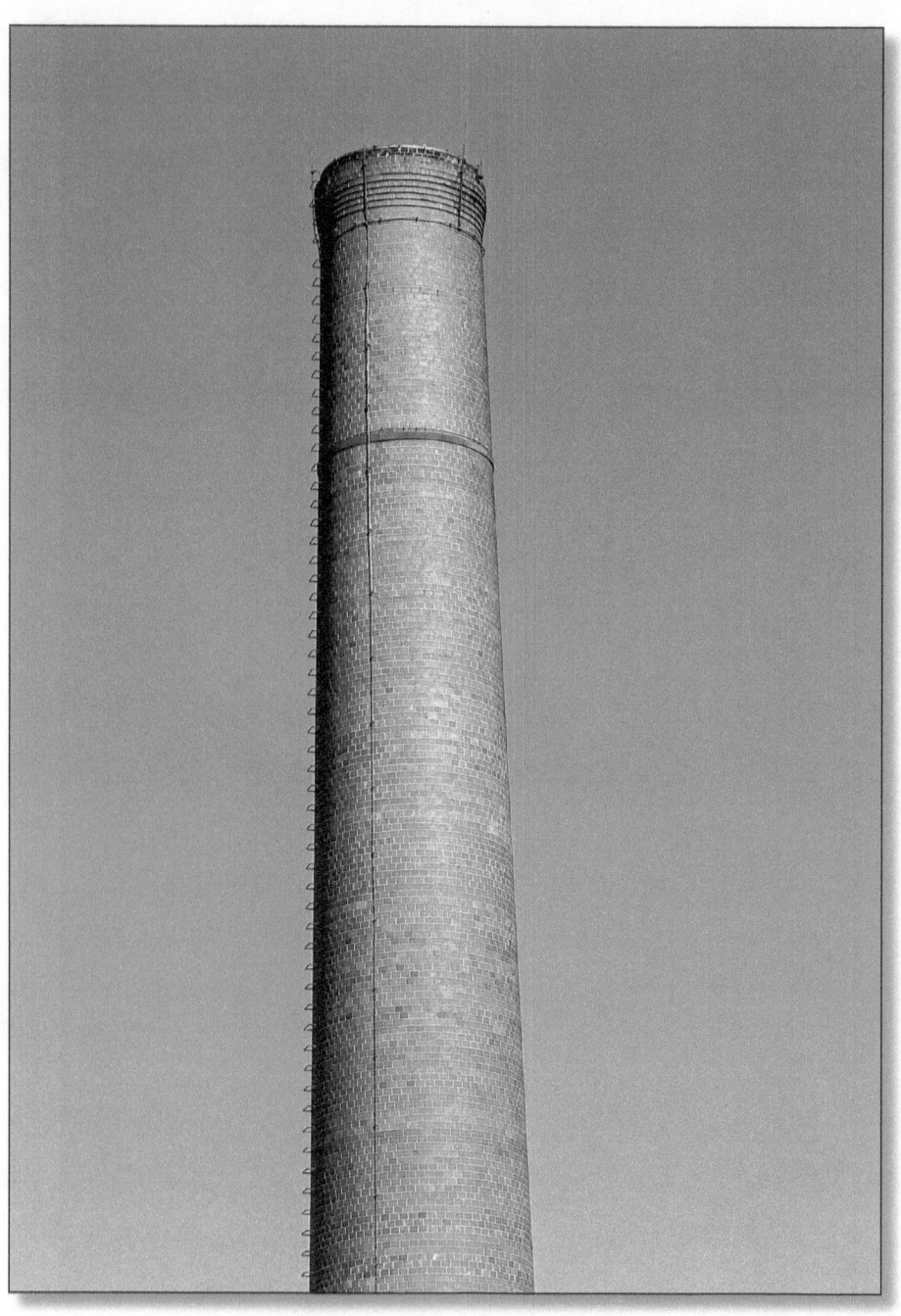

Ellis Hospital, Schenectady, N.Y., March 18, 2014.
Canon EOS 10D, 80mm, f/11, 1/650, ISO 200, P, pattern metering.
© 2014, 2015 by Shawn M. Tomlinson

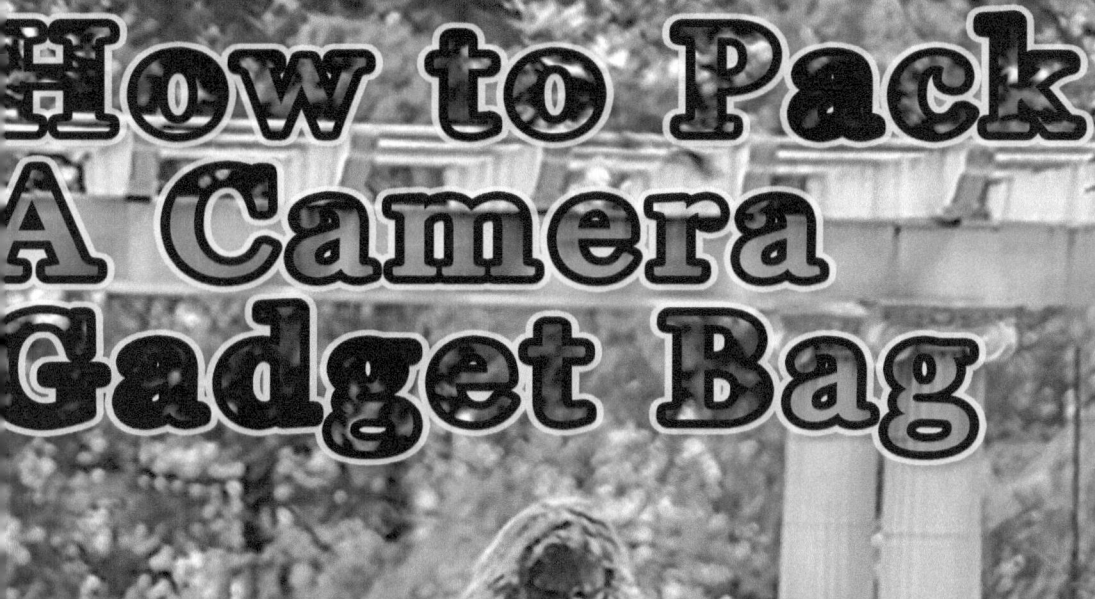

How to Pack A Camera Gadget Bag

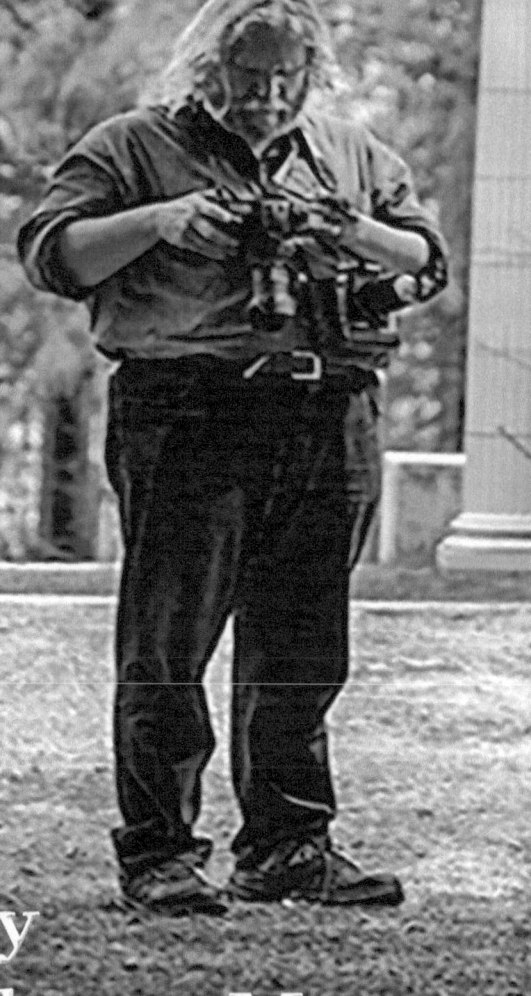

by

Shawn M.

Tomlinson

How to Pack A Camera Gadget Bag

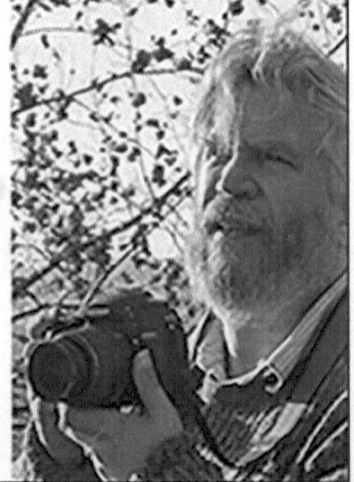

Shawn M. Tomlinson Photography

Art • Landscape • Profiles
Architecture • Studies
Commercial • Design

smtphotography62@gmail.com

How to Pack A Camera Gadget Bag

Every photographer needs a well-packed gadget bag.

Whether you're a hobbyist, wedding photographer, art photographer, travel photographer or something else, it's important to have everything you need in your gadget bag.

You may want to pack additional items, but here are some suggestions to get started.

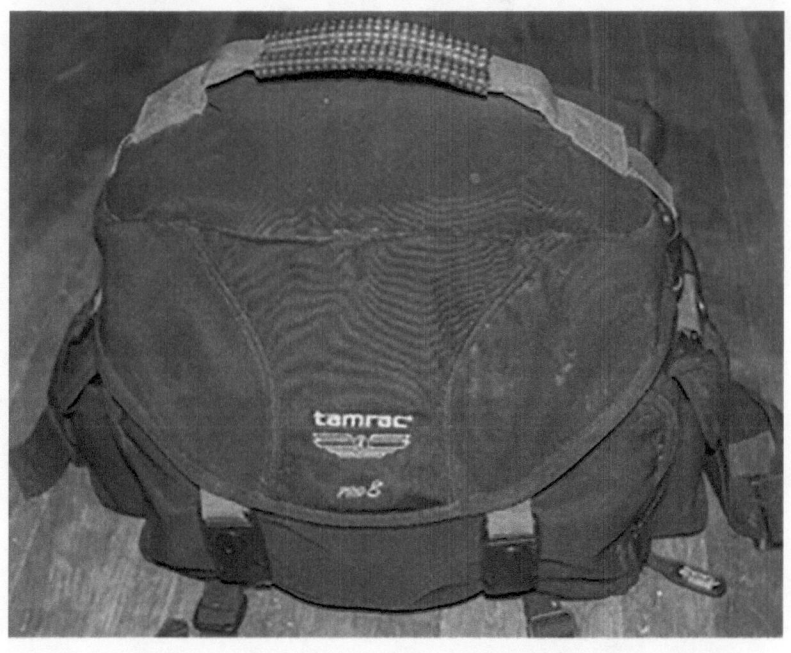

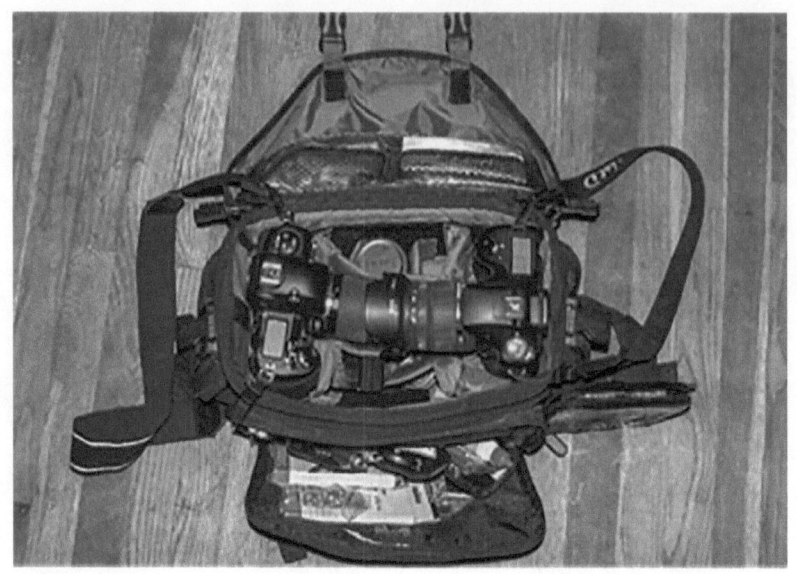

Serious amateur photographers or "enthusiasts" as the camera makers call them dream of gadget bags filled with the top, newest digital single-lens reflex cameras, drool at the prospect of filling those other spots with top-end lenses and, perhaps, having an assistant to carry it.

What exactly, though, goes into a gadget bag is something most people don't think about until they're out on a scenic, breathtaking, awe-inspiring mountain top and realize they missed something.

It pays to pack the gadget bag well because you may be someplace where you

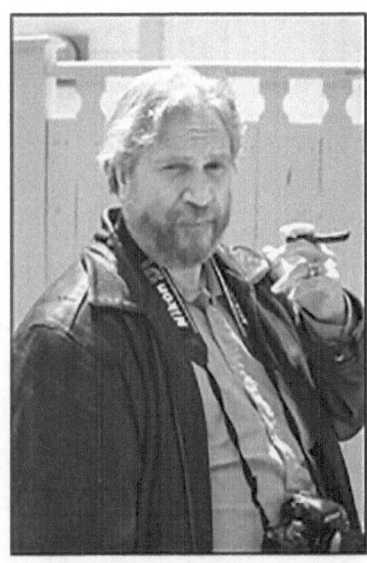

Photo by
Gary W. Ziroli

can't just pop into the local department store and buy what you forgot. Most major department stores don't even carry much of what you need anymore anyway in the stores so take it with you.

Here's how to pack a gadget bag for general photographic trip use. You may want to add or subtract things according to the kind of trip you're taking.

1) Camera body. OK, this first one is obvious, but we're packing the entire bag and we shouldn't leave out the DSLR. Most people only have one DSLR camera body, but if you own two, take both. It gives you a backup in case one camera dies or develops a fault. Of course, you'll need a big gadget bag for two DSLR bodies.

2) Lenses. Also obvious, but here's something to consider. If you own many lenses, you may not want to take them all because, depending on the type of trip, you may have to carry them all on your shoulder. If for example you own prime or fixed focal length wide-angle, normal and telephoto lenses, and wide-to-normal, normal-to-telephoto and telepho-to-to-super telephoto lenses, taking them all is going to be heavy. Think about what you really need.

A good sized gadget bag will hold all of the essentials for you as a photographer during your photo journeys. The basics include:

1) One or two DSLR camera bodies
2) Two to four lenses
4) Lens shades
5) Filters
6) Extra batteries
7) Memory cards
8) Battery charger
9) Flash
10) Snack

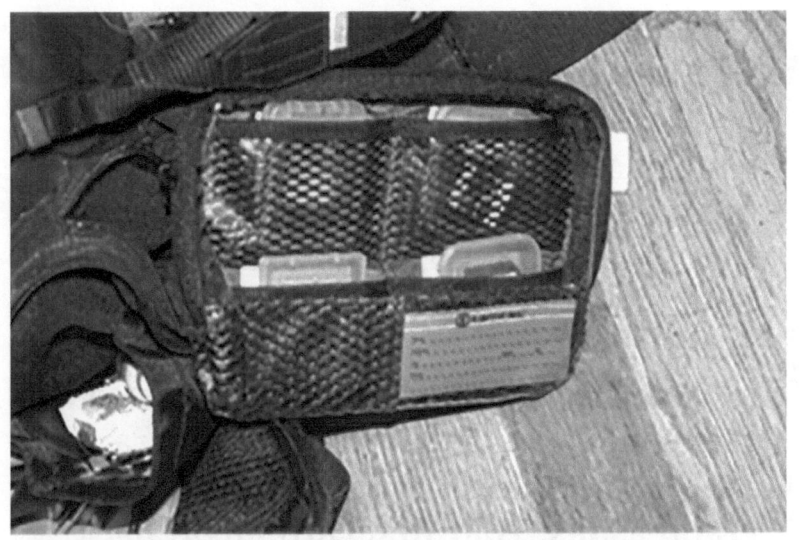

For example, if I'm going to a park, I probably will take a normal lens and a reasonable zoom, such as an 18-135mm. You're probably not going to need super telephoto unless you're planning to shoot wildlife. The normal lens gives great short focal depth and the same perspective as you see with your own eyes and as a prime lens, it's sharp.

The 18-135mm (for APS-C or crop-sensor DSLRs; for a full-frame camera, a 24-105mm) gives you good wide angle (27mm) shots as well as zooming up to 202.5 (on a crop-sensor DSLR). You don't really need the other lenses. You don't want to get tired and cut your photo shoot short.

3) Lens hoods. If you have them, lens hoods help to cut glare from the sun in your photos. You may not want to keep them attached to your lenses because they take up a lot of room that way, but off the lenses, they usually stack easily.

4) Memory cards. Of course you need the memory card that's in the camera, but you need to carry extra cards for several reasons. Your first card might pack it in the middle of your shoot and that would end it if you only have the one. Or, you might get so involved in the shoot you fill up the first memory card and want another one to keep shooting.

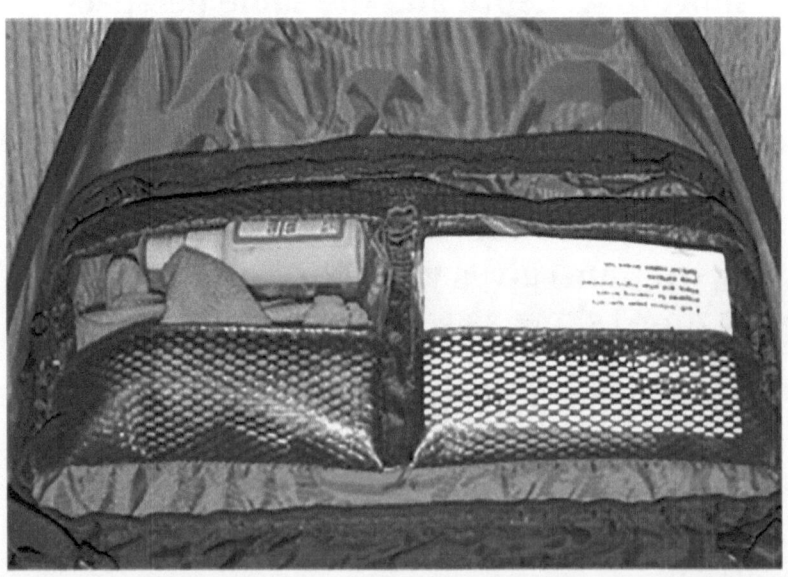

Lens caps are for amateurs. They get in the way and they only protect your lenses while they are on them.

5) Memory card reader. These are quite small these days and don't need a power source other than your computer. Keep one in your gadget bag and another in your computer case. Even if you have a MacBook Pro with a built-in SD card slot, having a card reader with you allows you to upload photos to other devices. Don't forget that tiny alternate USB cable for it.

6) Flash. Your DSLR probably has a popup fill flash on it, but you need a good bounce flash in your arsenal for situations where the fill flash won't fill. Bounce flashes are more versatile for photo shoots out of the studio than direct

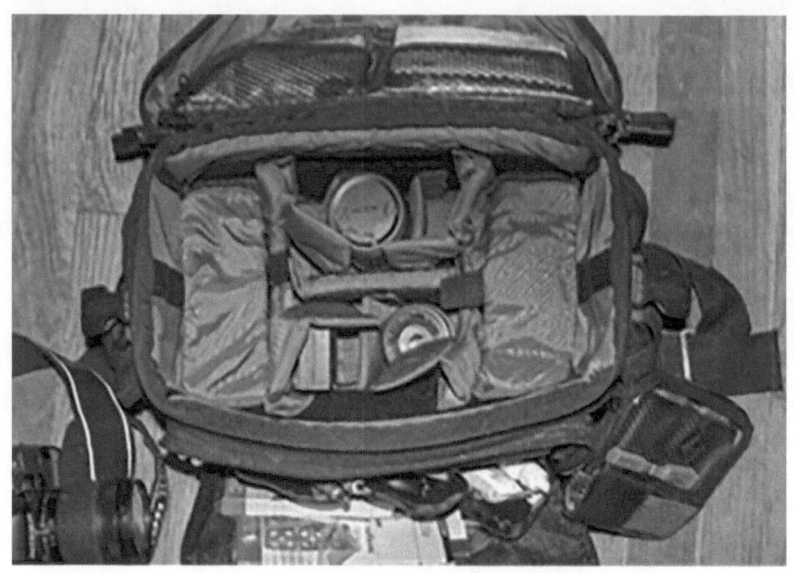

flashes because you can avoid harsh shadows. Don't forget extra batteries for your flash.

7) Batteries. If you shoot a lot, or even if you don't, you need at least one extra charged battery for your gadget bag. Batteries, like memory cards, can die. Carry at least one extra in the gadget bag. For added convenience, get a battery grip for your DSLR. This allows the use of two batteries without switching, effectively giving you twice the battery life.

8) Battery chargers. Keep at least one battery charger in your gadget bag at all times. It's true that you can't plug it in at

at the visitor center at the base of the mountain in the state park.

9) UV filters. Lens caps are for amateurs. They get in the way and they only protect your lens while they are on them. Every lens you have should have a UV or sky filter attached to the front at all times.

10) Polarizers. Polarizers give your images added depth, especially by deepening the blues in the sky. You can have one for each lens, or buy one big one and just hold it in front of each lens when you shoot. This sounds silly, but it works and saves money. You don't really need a polarizer, but it can add something to many photographs.

11) Lens tissue. The UV or sky filter can get dirty, so keep a pack of lens tissue handy to keep it clear.

12) Sensor cleaner. It's a bad idea to clean the sensor of your DSLR in the field, but sometimes it becomes necessary. If you change lenses often, dirt and dust are going to get on the sensor. If possible, sit down at a table indoors to

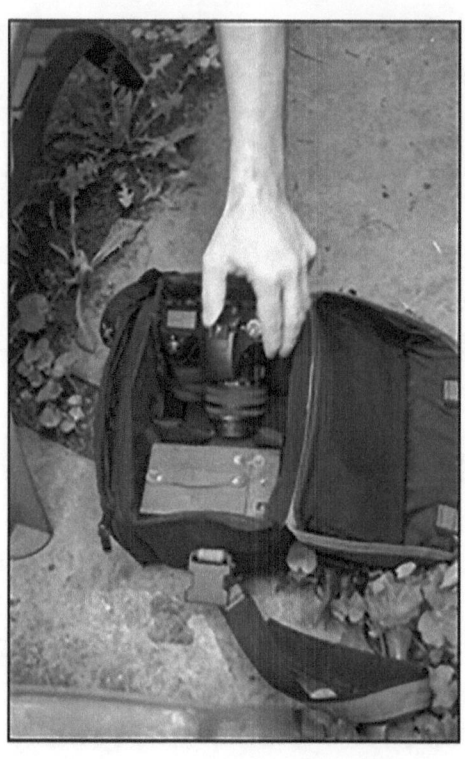

clean the sensor and be careful. It doesn't take a lot to damage the sensor.

Other stuff you may need:

1) Pencils and a notepad. Today's DSLRs record a great deal of data right in the files, and some DSLRs even allow you to record short notes to yourself to each image file. However, you may need to takes more extensive notes than this.

My first photography mentor told me as we drove to an assignment in 10-below temperatures that he always keeps regular old wooden lead pencils with him, along with a sharpener, because they never failed him. Pens don't work in really cold weather, and mechanical pencils have trouble with it, too.

2) Pocket poncho. These, basically, are plastic bags with holes cut in each for your head. You put it on over yourself and your DSLR too keep off the rain or snow. They're cheap and come folded small to fit in a gadget bag side pocket.

3) Remote control. If you have a battery grip on some DSLRs, you can tuck the remote control directly inside the grip for safe keeping. If not, keep it in your gadget bag. Remote controls can be used for self portraits, but also help when you need to make a long exposure or are using a long telephoto lens.

You can eliminate camera shake and cut down on motion blur in images by taking your hands off the camera and triggering the shutter with the remote control.

4) Snack bars. You might be on a photo shoot longer than you expect, and you might get hungry. Those small "fun size" candy bars you see at Halloween (and now all year) fit easily into the nooks and crannies of your gadget bag. If you are health conscious substitute granola or energy bars.

5) Name, address, phone number and email address. You might lose your gadget bag somewhere along the way dangling upside down from a cliff face, and some stranger may find it. On the off chance the stranger is honest and wants to get it back to you, give him or her the needed information. At the very least, the stranger may want to thank you for donating all that great camera equipment to him or her.

One thing that doesn't fit in most gadget bags — although some have tie-ons for it — is a tripod. Tripods are cumbersome and annoying, but they will give you rock-solid foundations to decrease or eliminate camera shake.

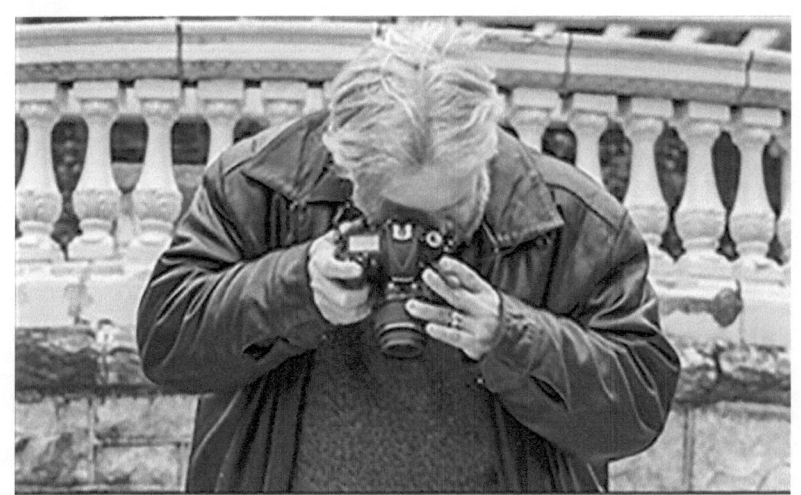
Photo by Gary W. Ziroli

About the Author

Shawn M. Tomlinson has been a photographer since 1976, professionally since 1982. He has worked in many newspapers as reporter, columnist, editor, photographer and designer. Tomlinson writes the Photo Curmudgeon column about photography, available in eBook editions on Amazon.com.

The author uses several gadget bags, but his main one is a Tamrac Pro 8 that currently holds his Nikon D7000 with battery grip and Nikon D70 DSLR camera bodies, a Nikon AF D 28mm f/2.8 prime lens, a Nikon G 18-55mm lens, a Tamron LD 70-300mm lens, a Nikon AF D 28-80mm lens, a Pentax flash, sensor cleaning kit, charger, naproxen sodium, Reese's FastBreak, "AA" batteries for the insert for the D7000 grip, pencils, pens, CF memory cards, SD memory cards, a polarizer and other assorted items.

How to Pack a Camera Gadget Bag

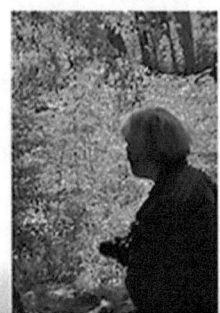

by shawn m tomlinson

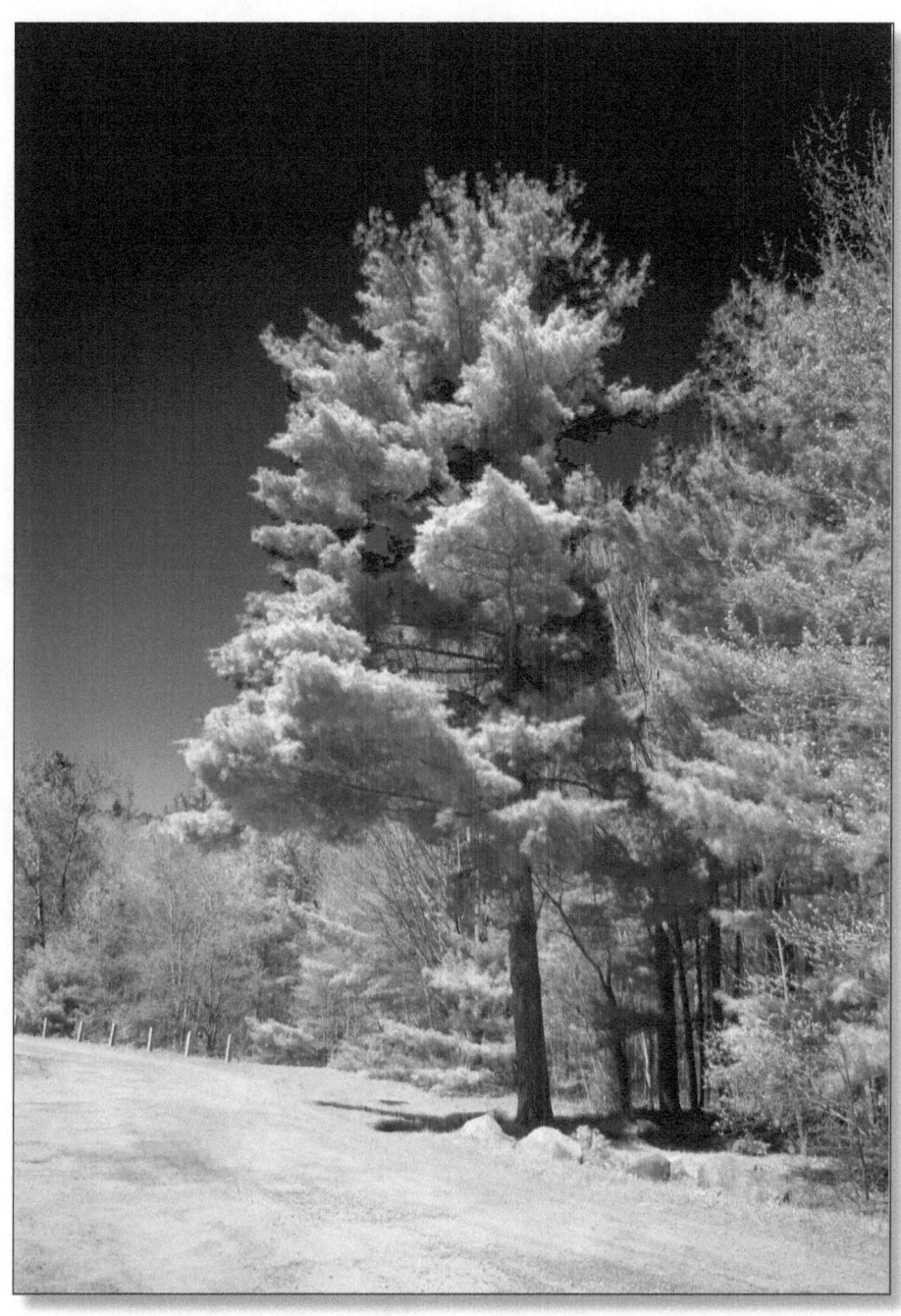

Boat Launch, Day, N.Y., May 5, 2013.
Pentax *ist DS, 18mm, f/4.5, 1/125, ISO 100, P, spot metering.
© 2014, 2015 by Shawn M. Tomlinson

Shawn M. Tomlinson's Guide to Photography Series

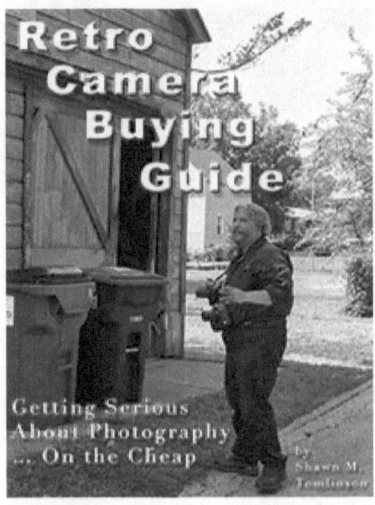

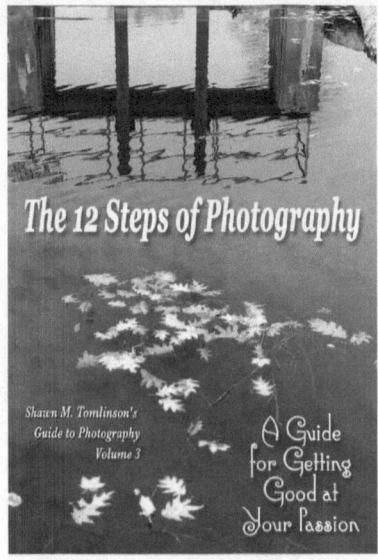

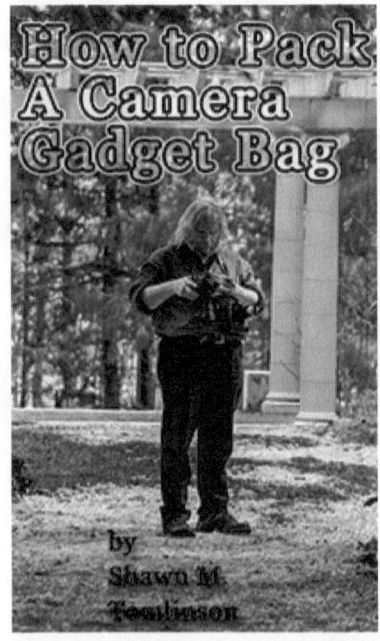

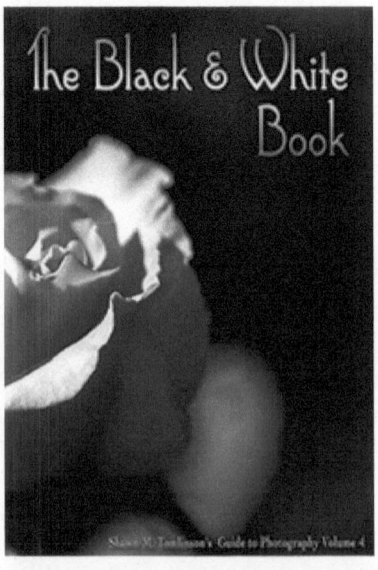

Shawn M. Tomlinson's
Guide to Photography Series

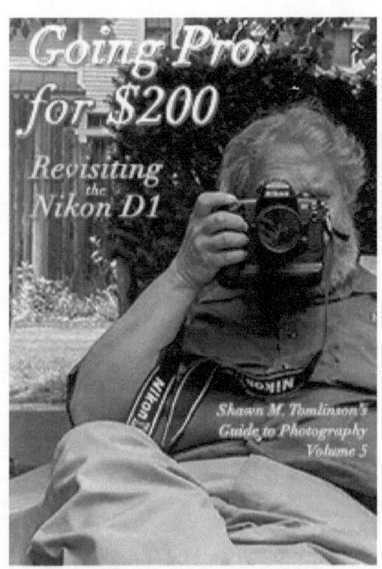

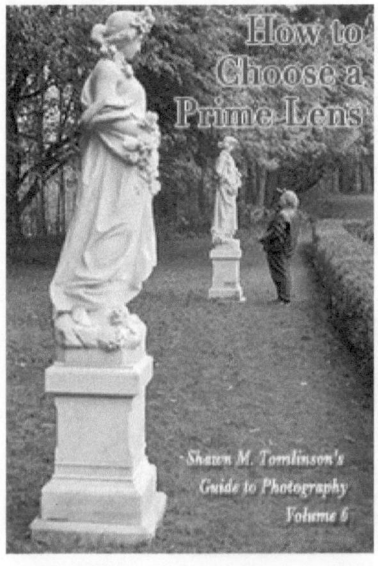

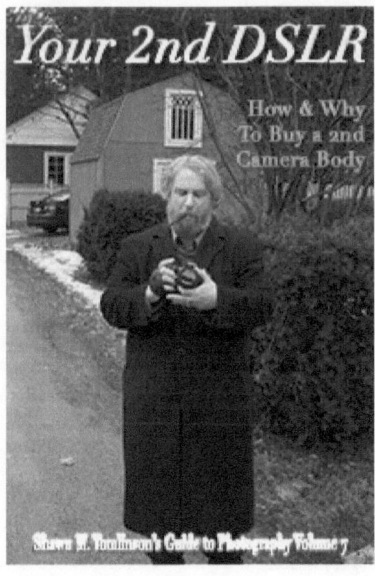

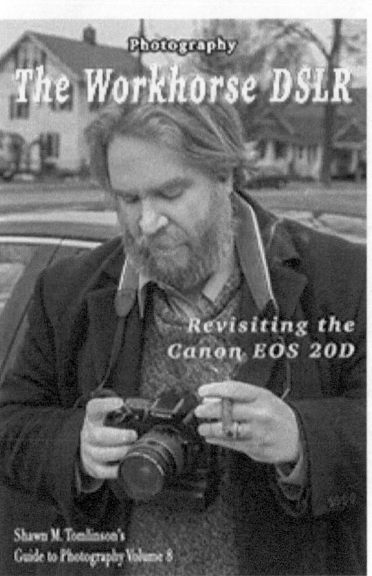

Shawn M. Tomlinson's Guide to Photography Series

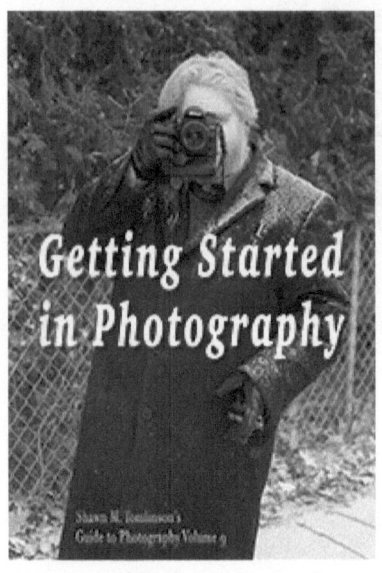

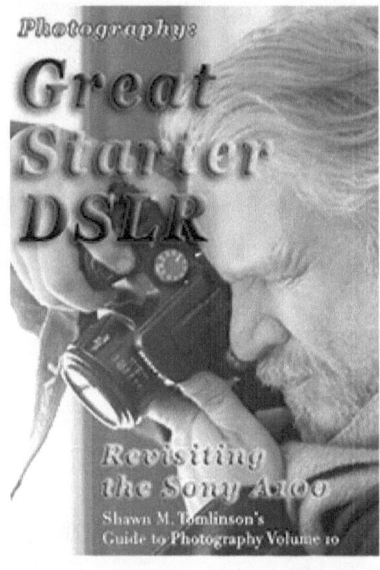

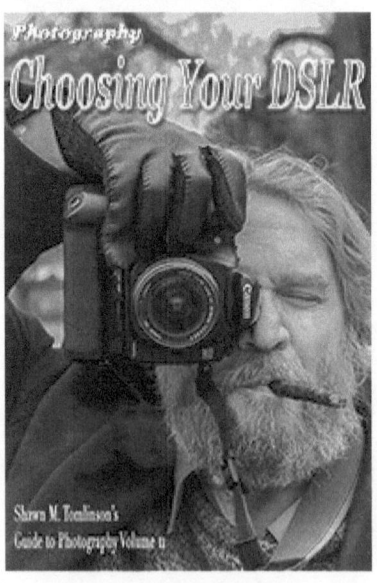

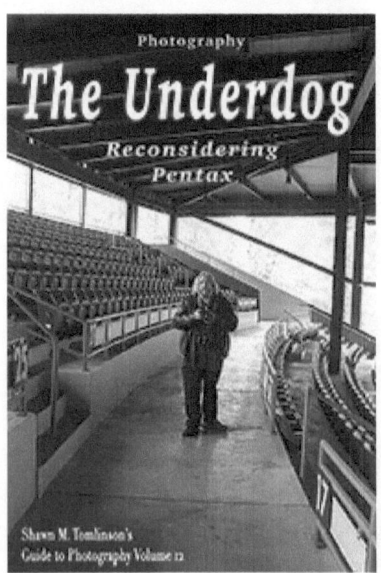

The Photo Curmudgeon

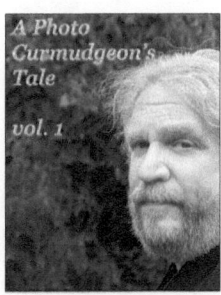

A Photo Curmudgeon's Tale Volume 1

The first 25 Photo Curmudgeon columns collection covering everything photographic also includes several columns that preceded the Curmudgeon. Includes many photographs to illustrate points in the columns.

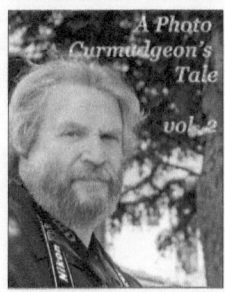

A Photo Curmudgeon's Tale Volume 2

The second 25 Photo Curmudgeon columns collection covering everything photographic considers lenses, cameras, photo editing techniques, locations and more.

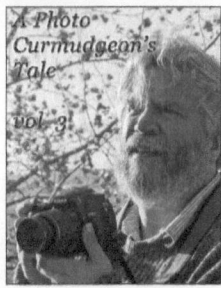

A Photo Curmudgeon's Tale Volume 3

Photo Curmudgeon columns 051-075 are collected in this third volume covering everything photographic including lenses, cameras, photo editing techniques, locations and more.

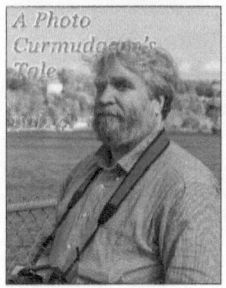

A Photo Curmudgeon's Tale Volume 4

Photo Curmudgeon columns 076-100 complete the fourth volume of the collection with insights about Nikon, Canon, Pentax DSLRs, prime lenses, seeking locations and technique among other topics.